(Opposite page) Thousands of Cast members gather in the Magic Kingdom to help kick off the "Tencennial" for Walt Disney World. The year-long tenth anniversary celebration began on October 1, 1981.

WALT DISNEY WORLD
The First Decade

Contents

The Vacation Kingdom
of the World

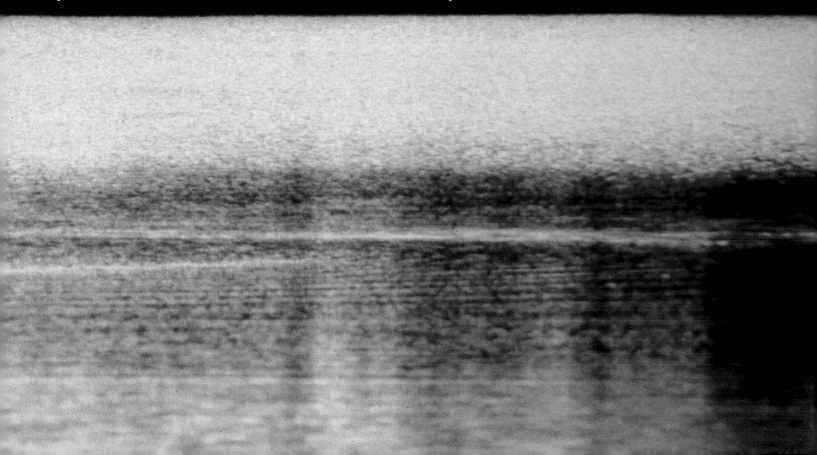

What is Walt Disney World? During the past ten years, nearly 126 million guests from more than 100 nations have come to Florida's heartland to discover the answer. And yet for every one of them, Walt Disney World is something different.

For grandparents, it's a nostalgic journey to Main Street, U.S.A. at the turn of the century. For toddlers, it's the joy of hugging Mickey Mouse or Winnie the Pooh. For the Huck Finn in all of us, it's splashing the day away in the gosh-darndest swimmin' hole this side of Hannibal, Missouri. And for science-fiction buffs, it's blasting off on a race through the cosmos in "Space Mountain."

It's youngsters enjoying the adventures of adulthood and parents joining in the pleasures of being a child. It's strangers sharing the common language of laughter. And being silly without embarrassment, knowing that like everyone else, they've escaped their everyday cares for the pursuit of dreams. As one guest put it, "It's people enjoying the best of what they are."

Walt Disney World is all these things and more. Whether guests come for two days, two weeks, or make it an annual tradition...they never run out of discoveries. The Vacation Kingdom is as rich as the imagination of Walt Disney himself.

"*Always Opening New Doors*"

"I believe the fun is in building something, in bringing new things to life. We never do the same thing twice. After we've finished a job . . . we head in another direction. We're always opening new doors."

—Walt Disney

Many call it "Disney's Folly" and predict that movie-goers won't pay to see it. But after three years in development, and with more than 1.5 million drawings used, Snow White and the Seven Dwarfs *becomes an artistic and financial triumph.*

Walt Disney (1947)

From the very beginning of his remarkable career, Walt Disney lived on the edge of tomorrow. Dreaming impossible dreams. And daring to make them come true.

A pioneer filmmaker, he was the first to make an animated "talkie," and the first to paint one with color. He developed the multi-plane camera to give his animated art a look of depth, then went on to unprecedented success with the first full-length animated feature, *Snow White and the Seven Dwarfs* (1937).

He introduced stereophonic sound to motion pictures with *Fantasia* (1940), and pioneered the projection of movies on a 360-degree screen with *Circle-Vision 360* in Disneyland (1955). Through his "Oscar"-winning *True-Life Adventures*, he expanded our knowledge of the wilderness, and through the antics of his unique cast of animated characters, he expanded our sense of humor.

With a weekly television show that debuted in 1954, Walt Disney gave American households what was to become the longest running "prime time" program in industry history. With the electronic wizardry of the Space Age, he gave lifelike movements to mechanical actors through the *Audio-Animatronics* system. And with his boundless imagination and determination, he gave life to "a magical little park" called Disneyland, one of the most important entertainment landmarks of the Twentieth Century.

While the Wizard's away, the Mouse will play... In the "Sorcerer's Apprentice" sequence of Fantasia, Mickey plays a neophyte magician who conjures up more of a spell than he can handle.

(Below left) Disguised as one of the herd, a Disney cameraman films buffalo for the "Oscar"-winning True-Life Adventure "The Vanishing Prairie" (1954). (Below) Walt Disney also premiers a weekly one-hour television program called Disneyland in 1954. On it he introduces his dream of a "Magic Kingdom" to the world. The TV program's title changes several times over the years (to Walt Disney in 1981), but as this book goes to press, the show remains the longest running "prime time" series in history.

During its first run from 1955-59, the Mickey Mouse Club TV show is viewed by more people than any other daytime program, and by more children than any other series—day or night—except Disneyland.

Walt Disney previews Disneyland concepts in 1954.

When Disneyland opened on July 17, 1955 in Anaheim, California, it was the realization of a 20-year-old dream for Walt Disney, its chief architect and leading "Imagineer."

"The idea came along," Walt said, "when I was taking my daughters around to those kiddie parks. While they were on the merry-go-round, riding 40 times or something, I'd be sitting there trying to figure out what I could do." It was those often unsatisfying afternoons that triggered the notion of a family park that would be as entertaining for adults as for their children.

"It took many years," Walt said. "I started with many ideas, threw them away, and started all over again. And eventually it evolved into what you see today at Disneyland."

Not an amusement park, and certainly not a kiddyland, Disneyland was like nothing the world had ever experienced.

To help create his "Magic Kingdom," Walt Disney had relied not on amusement park experts, but on filmmakers from his own Studio. In their hands, Disneyland was laid out like a gigantic outdoor stage, with sets dressed for comedy, drama and adventure. On each set, everything from architecture, landscaping and costumes, to food, music and sound-effects was orchestrated to the smallest detail, creating a totally "themed" environment.

The sets were "lands" to be entered and explored. Guests were not just spectators at a theatrical production, they were actual participants in the performance. When they strolled down Main Street, U.S.A., they relived hometown America at the turn of the century. When they boarded the "Jungle Cruise" in Adventureland, they journeyed to the outermost reaches of the world's densest jungles. In Frontierland, they traveled into the days of pioneer America; in Fantasyland, into the timeless world of Disney cartoon classics; and in Tomorrowland, into a world that may await voyagers of the future.

Public acceptance was overwhelming. Less than two years after the Magic Kingdom's opening, *Time* magazine said, "Thanks to Disney's pixilating power to strike the youthful nerve of Americans, Disneyland is proving to be America's biggest tourist attraction."

Disneyland was also hailed as the "greatest piece of urban design in the United States," drawing the praise of designers, architects and city planners from around the world. In a keynote address to the 1963 Urban Design Conference at Harvard University, James Rouse, a leading master planner and builder of new towns, said in part:

"I hold a view that may be somewhat shocking to an audience as sophisticated as this—that the greatest piece of urban design in the United States today is Disneyland... It took an area of activity—the amusement park—and lifted it to a standard so high in its performance, in its respect for people, in its functioning for people, that it really has become a brand new thing... I find more to learn in the standards that have been set and in the goals that have been achieved in the development of Disneyland than in any other single piece of physical development in the country."

Even with a phenomenal success and the praise of the world, Walt Disney was already planning an even greater entertainment innovation. At Disneyland's 10th Anniversary celebration in 1965, he cautioned his staff—"I just want to leave you with this thought, that it's just been a sort of dress rehearsal...if any of you start resting on your laurels, I mean just forget it..." Walt Disney was preparing to "imagineer" what was perhaps his greatest dream—Walt Disney World.

If Walt Disney had been able to step back in time and build Disneyland again, secure in the knowledge of its future success, he would surely have made one improvement. Somehow he would have managed to acquire more land.

(At upper left) On July 17, 1955,
Walt Disney dedicates Disneyland. On his left is California
Governor Goodwin Knight.
(Above) The "Showman of the
World" has the Sleeping
Beauty Castle drawbridge
lowered for the first—and last—
time, bringing a predictable
response from children eager to
visit Fantasyland.

When the Magic Kingdom opened in 1955, it
was an island of fantasy in an ocean of orange
trees. But guests were not all that the Park
attracted. Following the crowds were eager
speculators who quickly snatched up surrounding property. Hoping to catch some of
Disneyland's overflow, they cluttered the landscape outside the Magic Kingdom with fast-food
concessions, motels and counter-attractions.

Walt Disney watched this haphazard development, regretting that he had been financially
unable to provide Disneyland with an insulating
belt of greenery. Vowing that this would never
happen again, he turned his attention to building a new entertainment center somewhere in
the eastern United States.

By October 1965, Disney planners had
acquired nearly 27,500 acres right in the middle
of America's "sunshine state" and number-one
vacation mecca—Florida. That's 43 square miles,
an area twice the size of Manhattan Island or
equal in land area to all of San Francisco.

"There's enough land here to hold all the ideas and plans we can possibly imagine," Walt Disney said in announcing "Project - Walt Disney World." And incorporated into his Master Plan for the property situated near Orlando would be the dreams and philosophies of a lifetime.

With almost 150 times the acreage of Disneyland, it was clear that the Florida project would include much more than another Magic Kingdom. There would also be themed resort hotels and campsites, as well as a wealth of recreational activities, from boating to birdwatching to golf. Here, cushioned from the outside world, would be a complete "Vacation Kingdom," where families could visit for a day or easily spend a whole vacation together.

An impressive project to be sure, but in Walt Disney's Master Plan for the Florida property, it was only about the size of "super" in "supercalifragilisticexpialidocious." When Walt Disney came to Florida, he was looking far beyond his lifetime to the creation of an entire Experimental Prototype Community of Tomorrow—EPCOT—a showplace for new ideas and technologies from the creative centers of American industry, science and education. A place that would offer "blueprints" for a better life in the world of tomorrow.

Walt Disney died in 1966, shortly after introducing his concepts for the Florida project to the public. But the organization he had built, led by his brother Roy, plunged ahead with the development of the first phase of Walt Disney World, the vacation resort. The painstaking imagineering process continued for five years, transforming paintings, scale models and blueprints into a three-dimensional dream come true.

On October 1, 1971, the Vacation Kingdom of Walt Disney World opened to an eager public. One year and nearly 11 million guests later, it had already become one of the top-ranking vacation "nations" in the world—attracting more people in a year than the United Kingdom, Austria or Germany.

Now at the conclusion of its first decade, Walt Disney World stands as the premier vacation destination on Earth—enjoyed by nearly 126 million guests from more than 100 nations since its opening.

Today, Disney Imagineers are working full speed on the next phase of Walt Disney's plans for what one leading magazine called "The Entertainment Spectacular of the Century!" Epcot Center opens on October 1, 1982, featuring two major themed areas—Future World and the World Showcase.

The $800 million project will more than double the current $750 million investment in Walt Disney World, offering guests shows and adventures never before possible on such a grand scale. Epcot Center is expected to host eight to ten million guests during its inaugural year, and more than 100 million during its first decade.

At Epcot Center, guests will discover a 600-acre showplace for the innovations of tomorrow and the achievements of nations today. A showplace that Walt Disney predicted "more people will talk about and come to look at than any other place in the world."

Of course, Walt Disney World has been a home for innovative technologies since the beginning —as seen in the wealth of prototype systems at work behind the scenes, from a solar-powered office building to a vacuum-tube trash collection system. The Vacation Kingdom has also become a "crossroads of the world," evidenced by the guests attracted from around the globe by the magic of Disney entertainment.

This special-edition book is the story of Walt Disney World—from onstage and backstage. It is a reprise of its history, a look at its present success, and a preview of its boundless future. It is, however, a story without an ending. For Walt Disney's uncanny and fascinating ability to plan well into the future has ensured that a final chapter will never be written.

On the Vacation Kingdom site near Orlando, Florida, Walt Disney reviews plans with (from left) his older brother Roy O. Disney (then Chairman of the Board of Walt Disney Productions), E. Cardon Walker (then Vice President of Marketing for Walt Disney Productions, now Chairman of the Board), and Admiral Joe Fowler, administrator of the construction effort at Walt Disney World.

More than eight million cubic yards of earth are moved to construct Walt Disney World, and more than 8,000 workers representing every kind of building skill invade the site, often working around the clock. At the peak of construction in 1970, the Vacation Kingdom is the largest private construction project in the United States, and perhaps anywhere in the world.

The ornate Victorian buildings of Main Street, U.S.A., rise amidst a whirl of activities as Opening Day approaches. The attention lavished on even the most minute details ensures that guests will truly feel they are in another era.

Some 5,000 performers—not counting 500 doves released over the Magic Kingdom—join in the Grand Opening celebration and dedication ceremonies on October 25, 1971.

14

Roy O. Disney, Walt's older brother and business partner for more than 40 years, dedicates Walt Disney World.

(Above right) The first family to enter the Magic Kingdom at Walt Disney World on Opening Day, October 1, 1971, is Marty and Bill Windsor, Jr. from Lakeland, Florida, with their sons Jay and Lee. (Right) One thousand and seventy-six instruments are in the band led by "Music Man" Meredith Willson as part of the Grand Opening parade. Of course, there are 76 trombones.

The Magic Kingdom

At the heart of Walt Disney World is the Magic Kingdom. It's similar in design to Disneyland in California, but surrounded by lakes, resorts and miles of wilderness. Within the Magic Kingdom's sheltering, tree-covered berms are lands of fantasy and adventure, yesterday and tomorrow. Here, on a "time machine" called Imagination, you can escape your present-day world to stroll through a memory, or set sail on a dream for tomorrow.

"I don't want the public to see the world they live in while they're in the Park. I want them to feel they're in another world."

—Walt Disney
on the Art of
the Theme Show

MAIN STREET, U.S.A.

Walk through the Main Entrance and you're on Main Street, U.S.A., the first of six themed "lands" in the Magic Kingdom. It is the essence of hometown America at the turn of the century—the crossroads of an era, when the gas lamp was giving way to the electric light, and the sputtering horseless carriage was challenging Old Dobbin for the streetcar right-of-way.

Here, guests may sample homemade peanut brittle in the "Main Street Confectionery"... watch glass blowing and cutting in the "Crystal Arts"...have silhouettes created and framed while they wait in "The Shadow Box"...dine in Victorian elegance in the "Crystal Palace Restaurant"...thrill to silent-film stars at the "Main Street Cinema"...or simply enjoy an afternoon band concert in Town Square.

(At left) A passing musician joins in with the Banjo Kings.

18

(Below) Some 60 homing pigeons symbolizing doves of peace fill the late afternoon sky during the Flag Retreat Ceremony each day in Town Square. As the Flag is lowered and the Walt Disney World Band plays the National Anthem, the birds are released to make their dramatic flight over the Magic Kingdom.

19

The "Walter E. Disney," "Lilly Belle," "Roger E. Broggie" and "Roy O. Disney" are steam engines of the Walt Disney World Railroad. Originally built between 1915 and 1928, they hauled jute, sugar, hemp and passengers throughout the southernmost jungles of Mexico. In later years, they fell into disrepair. But after being purchased from the United Railways of Yucatan by Disney scouts, they were disassembled and shipped to the Gulf Coast for complete renovation. Now each steam engine pulls five open-sided passenger cars, departing from the Main Street Railroad Station for a one-and-a-half mile tour around the Magic Kingdom.

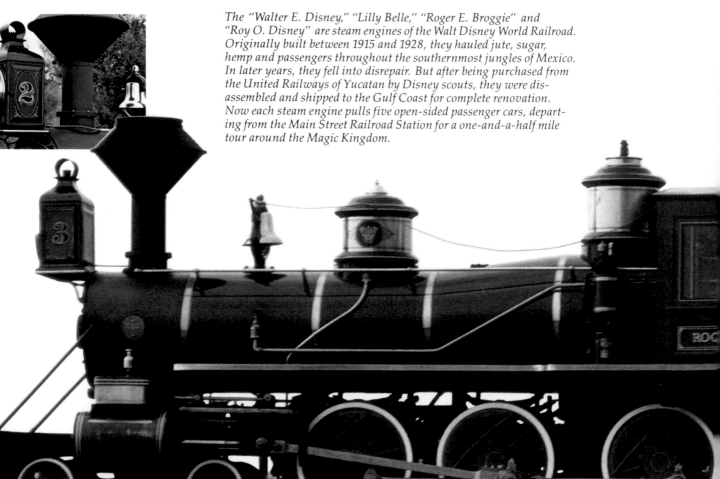

During a stop in Frontierland, the tender for a steam engine is filled with water from an old-fashioned wooden tower.

E. BROGGIE

WALT DISNEY WORLD R.R.

(Clockwise from upper left) Senator Hubert H. Humphrey takes time out from his 1972 presidential campaign to go for a spin with his family in a Main Street fire engine. The Firehouse is aglow with Victorian architectural detail. Sidewalk musicians stroll Main Street, entertaining passersby. When not cycling down the avenue, the Dapper Dans dispense harmony, humor and even a bit of fancy tap dancing, straight out of an era when men really did button spats over their shoes.

(At left) The Magic Kingdom version of City Hall provides information and assistance with reservations and transportation. (Below left) Located on Center Street, The Greenhouse offers silk flowers, lush green plants and decorative pottery. (Below) The Market House stocks the fun, food and flavor of a country store from the 1890s. Not to mention remedies by the jar-full for a youngster's sweet tooth.

(Above & upper right) Mickey and his friends join marching bands, colorful floats and characters from America's history in a patriotic salute for the U.S. Bicentennial—"America on Parade." (1976)

Mickey Mouse, the world's best known cartoon personality, turned 50 years young on November 18, 1978. It was the anniversary of his debut in Steamboat Willie, history's first sound cartoon. Here, "Mickey Mouse Superstar" and Minnie arrive at the Main Street Cinema, as admirers gather to honor the little fellow who reminded people how to laugh during the Depression Era, and who has kept us laughing ever since. Mickey's finest tribute, however, was delivered by Walt Disney himself, when he said of his Company, "I only hope that we never lose sight of one thing— that it was all started by a mouse."

(At left) More than a half-million twinkling lights, optical fibers and micro-neon threads trace fanciful characters, dancers and giant floats with light during the "Main Street Electrical Parade." This annual summertime spectacular premiered in June 1977.

(Above) On October 22, 1979, almost exactly eight years after Opening Day, a welcoming celebration is held for Kurt Miller of Kingsville, Maryland—the 100 millionth guest! (Below) During the Christmas season, Main Street sparkles like a jewel. A highlight of the holiday festivities is the annual Candlelight Procession, which fills the Magic Kingdom with the glow of a thousand candles and the music of a thousand voices. Carolers include local high-school students and Walt Disney World Cast members. In a dramatic finale, they create a living Christmas tree outside the Main Street Railroad Station, where The Night Before Christmas *is read by a noted personality. These special participants have included Cary Grant, Rock Hudson, Joe Campanella, Ross Martin and Perry Como.*

"The Miracle of the Hub"

The Magic Kingdom's most interesting design element is perhaps its overall layout. Main Street, U.S.A. is an entrance corridor—a sort of long "hallway" that can absorb many guests in a short time. The far end of Main Street, U.S.A. opens into a spacious central Plaza, or hub. From here, pathways fan out like the spokes of a wheel, leading to Adventureland, Frontierland, Liberty Square, Fantasyland and Tomorrowland. Each land features a visual centerpoint, and is easy to enter and exit.

"That gives people a sense of orientation," Walt Disney said. "They know where they are at all times [because all paths lead back to the Plaza], and it saves a lot of walking."

This unique "people-flow" system has sometimes been called the "miracle of the hub." The concept was introduced in the original design of Disneyland in California.

Topiary gardening—the sculpting of living shrubs into the shapes of animals, people or geometric designs—is an Old World art practiced at Walt Disney World. Each topiary figure is designed, grown and groomed by a special team of Disney gardeners. A topiary spends at least five years in the Tree Farm at Walt Disney World before making its debut.

Nature is a colorful artistic partner in imagineering. Bright blossoms appear in everchanging patterns the year 'round throughout the Magic Kingdom. Along the Plaza, topiary figures gently accent the formal Victorian gardens and walkways. (At right) Twilight settles over the Plaza, and "fireflies" shimmer in the trees.

While being concerned about easy access to all areas of the Magic Kingdom, Disney Imagineers took great care to give the Park a sense of continuity. Like a motion picture, the Disney Theme Show takes its audience through carefully structured scene changes designed to tell a story. All the elements within a themed land work together to create a smooth and consistent chain of events, and each land relates to the others in a non-competitive way. Contradictions that would intrude upon what the story seeks to communicate have been studiously avoided.

In contrast, as a key Disney Imagineer explained, "One of the worst things about most traditional amusement parks [and, for that matter, most commercial development] is that every

An area just off the central Plaza, between Main Street, U.S.A. and Adventureland, illustrates how two seemingly disparate environments—a Victorian street and a tropical jungle—are made to flow smoothly from one to the other. This transitional setting is the home of the "Crystal Palace Restaurant." It's reminiscent of the Victorian conservatories built during the 19th Century, when the British Empire spread its language, culture and architectural styles around the globe.

Consequently, the elegant restaurant fits as comfortably into a 19th Century British West African setting (a region and time depicted in sections of Adventureland), as it does on a Victorian Main Street. Many guests are never consciously aware of this subtle transition, but they feel a shift in mood. While they tend to stroll leisurely down Main Street, U.S.A., their pace quickens when they enter Adventureland.

Similar transitions abound throughout the Magic Kingdom. By orchestrating architectural styles, building heights, landscaping, colors, graphics, materials, sound, and many other elements, the Disney Theme Show is brought to life.

facility tries to outshout the others. People are subject to pressures from one exhibit, as opposed to a second, as against a third. It makes for mental fatigue. You pick up one idea, then drop it completely as you go on to another area. By the end of the day, most people are absolutely exhausted and can't remember very much of what they've seen. The attractions have cancelled each other out."

Just off the Plaza between Main Street, U.S.A. and Adventureland, guests may dine in Victorian splendor at the Crystal Palace Restaurant. The Victorian, yet tropical character of the restaurant helps create a smooth visual transition between the two themed lands. There is an extensive use of glass, traditional brass fittings and colorful stained-glass windows in the Crystal Palace. The sun-filled atrium is reminiscent of the elegant British conservatories of the late 1800s. The towering palm tree was lowered by a crane through the roof during the restaurant's construction.

Cinderella
Castle

The gateway to Fantasyland is "Cinderella Castle." The tallest structure in the Magic Kingdom, it soars more than 180 feet, with golden spires rising majestically against an azure sky. Inspired by dreams and fortified with 276 tons of steel, the castle was built to last forever—a crowning symbol for all of the Magic Kingdom.

Like most Magic Kingdom architecture, Cinderella Castle deliberately reflects a romantic vision, inspired by several architectural styles and not by any one set of Old World blueprints. Though idealized and dreamlike, it captures the evolution of castle design in Europe during the Middle Ages.

The castle base is monumental, resembling a medieval fortress of the 13th Century. But as the structure rises, it becomes lighter and lacier—more like a palace of the Renaissance, saluting the craftsmanship of an age when the arts in Europe flourished.

La Fontaine de Cendrillon, *created in bronze, is named for the fairytale heroine who first became popular in France in 1697, and later inspired the 1950 Disney animated classic* Cinderella.

Artistry and craftsmanship also find expression inside the castle, where five mosaic panels depicting scenes from the *Cinderella* fairy tale adorn the foyer walls. The panels took more than two years to complete and contain hundreds of thousands of jewel-like pieces of Italian glass in more than 500 colors. Many of the pieces were hand-cut, with some bits as small as the head of a tack, while others were fused with silver and 14K gold.

The results would dazzle a fairy godmother. But the mosaics are only a sample of the castle's infinite detail. The Disney family crest is carved

above the Gothic entrance. Hinges on the castle doors are ornate recreations of a 15th Century style. Atop each supporting column are sculpted characters from the Disney motion picture *Cinderella*. In "King Stefan's Banquet Hall," hand-stitched medieval banners hang high above diners. Among the castle's spiraling towers, finely detailed gargoyles leer from lofty perches.

Few guests are ever consciously aware of all these creative touches. Taken individually, they are only small jewels in the castle's crown. But collectively, they add up to a visual feast that is the true art of the Disney Theme Show.

Guests dine amid medieval splendour in King Stefan's Banquet Hall on the upper floor of Cinderella Castle.

33

It took four years of research, design and construction to bring Cinderella Castle from dream into reality.

Cinderella Castle is a dramatic backdrop as President Jimmy Carter addresses 3,000 delegates to the 26th World Congress of the International Chamber of Commerce in 1978. It is the first time that the congress meets outside of a host nation's capital city. In a lighter moment during his speech, President Carter remarks—"I was looking forward to seeing Fantasyland, particularly because it is the source of inspiration for my economic advisors." (At right) Highlighting the Walt Disney World Grand Opening in 1971 is Arthur Fiedler conducting the World Symphony Orchestra in front of Cinderella Castle. The 142-member orchestra included representatives from every major symphony orchestra in the United States and 57 other nations.

Every attraction, shop and restaurant in the Magic Kingdom offers a seemingly unlimited wealth of intricate detail. Throughout the Magic Kingdom, there are more than 25,000 one-of-a-kind signs. Yet Disney graphics designers may invest weeks of work on just one, making certain that it enhances the mood of its location.

A list of every design element in the Magic Kingdom would probably fill the pages of an unabridged dictionary. But what is even more impressive is the way that these elements are arranged. Like the right combination of words, the results are often poetry.

Fantasyland

In Fantasyland, guests participate in the action of three-dimensional scenes derived from Walt Disney's animated classics. Attractions include "Peter Pan's Flight," "Snow White's Adventures" and "Mr. Toad's Wild Ride."

By crossing the drawbridge of Cinderella Castle, guests enter Fantasyland, "The Happiest Kingdom of Them All." This timeless land of enchantment is dedicated to those who believe that when you wish upon a star, your dreams really can come true.

There are ten major Fantasyland attractions, most of them based on Walt Disney's animated classics. These motion pictures, like the ancient folk tales that inspired them, never grow old. They have been enjoyed worldwide by generation after generation of movie-goers for more than 40 years.

In Fantasyland, guests can take a scary trip through the Enchanted Forest and Diamond Mine seen in *Snow White and the Seven Dwarfs*. *Peter Pan* contributes a flight in a pirate galleon high above the moonlit streets of London Town on a journey to Never Land. J. Thaddeus Toad's motorcar roars out of *The Adventures of Ichabod and Mr. Toad* to take guests for a wild ride along the road to "Nowhere in Particular." And the

When famous faces meet at Walt Disney World, laughter often follows. (Far left) Carol Channing, star of Broadway, is certain that diamonds are a girl's best friend. Now, if she could just figure out whether this is Chip or Dale? (1978) (Left) Susan Ford, daughter of President Gerald R. Ford, enjoys the antics of her Magic Kingdom friends in 1976.

people-sized cups and saucers whirling about are "spin-offs," so to speak, of the Mad Hatter's Tea Party in *Alice in Wonderland.*

While exploring Fantasyland, guests encounter a host of familiar characters—Winnie the Pooh, Captain Hook, Dopey, Sneezy, Doc and countless others. None, however, is more universally recognized than the one born in Walt Disney's imagination more than 50 years ago.

In this character's youth, he was a tiny figure drawn from simple circles, with rubber-hose limbs and a mischievious snout. But these were to be the dimensions of a superstar. His unmistakable image has become one of the most well-known around the world during this century. He is, of course, Mickey Mouse.

Among the Disney stars who greet guests in Fantasyland are Mickey Mouse and Snow White.

37

Created by some of the world's most skilled wood-carvers in 1917, "Cinderella's Golden Carrousel" was in disrepair when found by Disney scouts at a park in Maplewood, New Jersey during the 1960s.

Measuring 60 feet in diameter, it proved to be one of the largest carrousels ever built. Beneath thick layers of paint covering the horses, artisans discovered elaborate detail surviving in gleaming wood.

Disney designers replaced a few stationary chariots on the carrousel with additional galloping horses, raising the number of steeds from 72 to 90. Each horse was then painted in a unique, brilliant color scheme, highlighting its individual design. To complement Cinderella Castle, Imagineers topped the carrousel with a gold and white canopy, inspired by the tournament tents of medieval knights. Around the outer face of the canopy, 18 hand-painted vignettes detail scenes from the Walt Disney motion picture Cinderella.

The carrousel now receives meticulous daily care. As the focal point of Fantasyland's castle courtyard, it is a splendid tribute to a lost turn-of-the-century art...and a never-ending source of joy for millions who gallop the handsome white steeds.

(Left) While aboard the "Skyway to Tomorrowland," which departs from a Swiss chalet in Fantasyland, guests sail over the Pinocchio Village Haus, a restaurant where dining takes on a storybook charm.

The children of the world take would-be globetrotters on the happiest cruise that ever sailed. Originally created for the 1964 New York World's Fair, "It's A Small World" is Walt Disney's salute to the happy spirit of children everywhere. One Magic Kingdom guest wrote, "In view of all our international turmoil, I feel that our planet's confused verbal combatants would not take themselves so seriously if they would take time to visit It's A Small World."

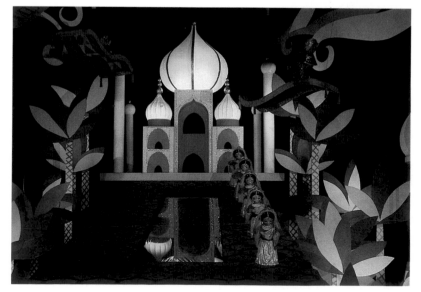

Timothy Mouse directs the action as guests soar high above Fantasyland aboard "Dumbo the Flying Elephant," an attraction inspired by Walt Disney's animated classic of 1941.

Nadia Comaneci, the 15-year-old darling of the 1976 Montreal Winter Olympics, takes a break from gymnastics during a 1977 exhibition tour of the U.S.A. to visit Walt Disney World with her Rumanian teammates. Said one official, "It's probably one of only five days they'll have off all year."

41

A 38-passenger "Nautilus"-style submarine makes an overland trip from California to the Magic Kingdom in Florida. It's one of 12 submarines that cruise the mysterious underwater world of "20,000 Leagues Under the Sea."

Along with Walt Disney's animated films, one of his classic live-action features becomes three-dimensional in Fantasyland. From the Cinderella Castle courtyard, guests may chart a course to Vulcania—Captain Nemo's South Seas hideaway in *20,000 Leagues Under the Sea*, based upon the Jules Verne science-fiction adventure.

Submarines styled after the "Nautilus" sail from a peaceful tropical lagoon on a journey through coral reefs to a vast sunless cavern, descending into an ocean of untold mysteries.

Of course, as every guest soon learns, things are not always what they appear to be in the Magic Kingdom. The breathtaking aquatic landscapes created for "20,000 Leagues Under the Sea" are a good example. Equipped with steel, stucco, fiberglass, a small fortune in gold leaf and a rainbow of epoxy paints, Disney artisans worked magic, transforming an 11.5 million gallon "pool" into an incredible underwater wonderland. With steel, lathe and plaster, they fashioned icebergs and cavernous rock formations. They turned engineered materials into sea grass, kelp, garlands, giant clams, seahorses and every type of coral imaginable.

Not all the scenery is illusionary, however. Mixed with the imagineered reproductions is a vast array of very real artworks by Nature—corals, shells, minerals and so on. Yet the Disney sealife is so authentic, it has been known to fool the very artisans who created it. Occasionally, one may even see real divers—Disney maintenance personnel—working beside the *Audio-Animatronics* members of an undersea farming crew.

In addition to viewing mysteries of the ocean depths in 20,000 Leagues Under the Sea, Magic Kingdom guests may explore rivers in the world's densest jungles. The cruise begins in Adventureland, our next stop in the Magic Kingdom.

ADVENTURELAND

When creating Adventureland, Disney Imagineers strove to make it "a wonderland of Nature's own design." And to anyone who journeys through this exotic land, it is obvious that the direction was followed leaf, stalk and petal.

A veritable United Nations of plants was assembled to represent tropic regions of the world. From the South Pacific to the West Indies, from darkest Africa to the densest Amazon, flowering

(Clockwise from right) At the Adventureland Veranda, guests may dine on Polynesian-styled entrees in a tropical setting. The brisk rhythms of a steel drum band bring heartbeats of the Caribbean to Adventureland. The Veranda Juice Bar is a thirst-quenching oasis for explorers.

trees radiate the spectrum in brilliant, ever-changing patterns of blossoms. Vigorously twining vines and vast stands of bamboo, palms, ferns and grasses add contrasting textures and cooling shades of green.

The landscapes look so natural that it's easy to overlook the human effort behind their creation. Yet at one time, the Magic Kingdom site was as barren and flat as a tabletop.

When Walt Disney purchased his Florida property in the middle 1960s, he found that major portions were sandy marshland. The challenge for the Disney team was to make the land stable enough to support construction. Draining the site was out of the question, since that procedure historically had proven disastrous to Florida's delicate ecology. Rather than lower the water table, it was decided to raise the elevations of the construction areas, leaving the environmental quality of the overall site undisturbed.

The Magic Kingdom was to be built atop an elevated "platform," using stabilized landfill sturdy enough to support construction. Unfortunately for Disney landscape architects, this "ground work" created an almost impervious layer of clay reaching depths of 14 feet.

For trees to survive, it was necessary to excavate generous pits and borings through the clay to the natural grade. The holes were then filled with sand and a special soil mix that permitted vertical drainage and healthy root development.

The clay was only one of many landscaping obstacles. Across large sections of the Magic Kingdom site, landfill had to be cleared to accommodate a vast service facility housed in a network of underground tunnels. If the trees above the tunnels had not been placed in specially devised planters, their roots would have hung from subterranean ceilings like chandeliers.

Workers attach fabricated leaves and flowers to the branches of a steel and stucco tree, transforming it into a huge, natural-looking setting for the "Swiss Family Treehouse." Like many Walt Disney World attractions, the Treehouse presented special challenges to designers and engineers. It was a one-of-a-kind creation, unlike any studied in architectural or engineering schools, and it had to comply with stringent construction codes for public buildings.

(Clockwise from left) An ingenious bamboo conveyance system supplies the "Swiss Family Treehouse" with a constant supply of fresh water. The Treehouse furnishings, including a pump organ and ship's wheel, are items that the Swiss Family Robinson salvaged from their ill-fated vessel in the 1960 Disney motion picture. Millions of guests have ascended rough-hewn steps to explore this fascinating tree-top home.

Walt Disney World abounds with landscaping feats. Challenges have been met with an array of inventive solutions. From the manicured Victorian gardens of Main Street, U.S.A. to the soaring pines of the Frontierland wilderness, the landscapes are "living backdrops" for the Magic Kingdom's stages, dressed with ever-changing colors and forms.

To plant one special tree in Adventureland, however, Disney landscape architects had to defer to the skills of show designers and engineers. The "Swiss Family Treehouse," inspired by the Disney motion picture *Swiss Family Robinson*, is nestled high up in the limbs of what may be the largest engineered tree in the world; rivaled only by a sister tree at Disneyland in California.

Since it was impossible to transplant a living specimen large and strong enough to support the multi-level treehouse, Disney Imagineers created a 200-ton steel and stucco counterpart. Immense concrete roots penetrate 42 feet into the ground, and 800,000 vinyl flowers and leaves "grow" on 600 branches spreading 90 feet wide. This rare species has been unofficially christened *Disneyodendron eximius*—"out-of-the-ordinary Disney tree."

(Top) The plant life seen on the "Jungle Cruise" is really a series of mini-jungles, with foliage in each area suggesting a specific tropical region of the world. (Above) King Hussein of Jordan embarks on the Jungle Cruise in 1975.

Some of the most out-of-the-ordinary sights encountered in Adventureland are on the "Jungle Cruise." Inspired by Walt Disney's highly acclaimed *True-Life Adventures*, the Jungle Cruise is a favorite attraction among armchair travelers. It compacts into ten minutes the highlights, mystique, fun and excitement of an adventure that could only be duplicated through weeks on safari. Best of all, it has none of the mosquitoes, monsoons and other misadventures of the "not always so great" outdoors.

This brand of "spruced-up" reality is integral to the Disney Theme Show. As a key designer said, "The environments we create are more utopian, more romanticized, more like the guests imagined they would be. For the most part, negative elements are discreetly eliminated, while positive aspects are in some cases embellished to tell the story more clearly."

(Clockwise from left) An ancient Asian shrine is discovered along the banks of the Irrawaddy River on the "Jungle Cruise." Elsewhere during their adventure, explorers are challenged by fearsome natives and delighted by playful elephants.

The original plans for Walt Disney World did not include a "Pirates of the Caribbean" attraction, because it was thought that Florida was already close enough to the real location. However, countless guests who had enjoyed the adventure at Disneyland in California adamantly disagreed. The attraction premiered at Walt Disney World in December 1973, climaxing a 50th Anniversary celebration for Walt Disney Productions.

"Pirates of the Caribbean," located in Adventureland's Caribbean Plaza, clearly embodies this utopian spirit. The storyline portrays a disaster—the capture, pillaging and ultimate burning of a seacoast town by a crew of swashbucklers who would shiver the timbers of Blackbeard. Yet scurrilous as they are, there is something loveable about these rapscallion rogues. And while their captives may fret a little, they seem to be having as much fun as the buccaneers.

Beyond the Caribbean Plaza lies Frontierland. Like a voyage through Pirates of the Caribbean, a visit to Frontierland is a step back into history, only now the destination is pioneer America.

The Frontierland border near Adventureland is reminiscent of Southwest America around 1880. Spanish in flavor, it features design elements also found in the Caribbean Plaza. Red tile roofs and stucco walls, for example, are architectural details common to both areas. This similarity in architectural styles enabled Disney designers to establish a smooth visual transition between Adventureland and Frontierland. Before we know it, we are out of the tropics and into the Great American Frontier.

(Upper left) Like all areas of the Magic Kingdom, Caribbean Plaza reflects the skill of Disney designers in portraying other times and places. Meandering walkways, hidden courtyards, tile-lined fountains and pastel buildings grace an outdoor bazaar as picturesque as any on the Spanish Main. (Upper right) Two-hundred and twenty-five singing birds, crooning flowers and chanting tiki gods fill the Sunshine Pavilion with the happy sounds of "Tropical Serenade." When the musical-comedy revue reaches its peak, the celebration is suddenly halted by a violent thunderstorm unleashed by angered island gods. (Above) A towering thatched-roof pagoda stands at the entrance to the Sunshine Pavilion, which is styled after a South Seas assembly lodge. (Left) Julie Nixon Eisenhower tours Adventureland with a group of Girl Scouts in 1973.

Frontierland

All Americans, whether tenth-generation or naturalized citizens, have cause to be proud of their nation's history, shaped by the pioneering spirit of its founders. It is to those hardy pioneers, men and women of vision, faith and courage, that Frontierland is dedicated.

In designing this themed land and its neighbor, Liberty Square, Disney Imagineers telescoped America's great westward expansion—from the Atlantic to the Pacific and from the 1770s to the 1880s—into one Magic Kingdom panorama. Subtle changes in scenery along the way belie shifts in eras and locales.

When entering Frontierland from Adventureland, guests first pass a desert setting reminiscent of America's great Southwest. From here to the "Colorado Plateau," what follows is truly one of the most remarkable landscapes ever to rise out of the Florida flatlands.

First, bend iron rebar into the general shapes of weathered buttes and place the assembled pieces over a monumental steel base. Then stretch lathe over the rebar to further define rock surfaces, and to serve as a foundation for the "mud" that will be applied to give the rocks a rough texture. Then apply color. Now you've built a mountain, or in this case, Big Thunder Mountain.

Rising 197 feet and spanning two acres, Big Thunder Mountain is the tallest "mountain" in Florida. So convincing are the rusty hues of weathered and eroded rock in the mountain, an observer could easily be fooled into perceiving natural elements. Big Thunder might well have been towering above the Florida flatlands for millenia.

"Big Thunder Mountain Railroad," the Magic Kingdom's newest attraction, opened in Frontierland in 1980. Its towering buttes appear to be straight out of Monument Valley, Utah, and look so real, they just might confuse a geologist. They are a testament to the ability of the Disney team to create rockwork that looks as though it has been weathering naturally for thousands of years.

Ten years of planning and 18 months of construction went into Big Thunder, not to mention 650 tons of steel, 4,675 tons of specially-formulated "mud" and more than 9,000 gallons of paint. At $17 million, Big Thunder's cost equaled that of Disneyland at its 1955 opening. More than $300,000 alone was spent on authentic set decorations, including an ore-hauling wagon, wooden mining flume, "double-stamp" ore crusher, and old mill ball.

(Right) Singer John Davidson, his daughter Jennifer, and "Cowboy Mickey" experience the runaway excitement of "Big Thunder Mountain Railroad" on its inaugural run in 1980.

Aboard Big Thunder Mountain Railroad, guests are whisked back into the Gold Rush for "the wildest ride in the wilderness!" Runaway mine trains race around towering buttes into foreboding caverns filled with phosphorescent pools and dark chasms. Narrow escapes come rapid-fire. The reckless trains careen past raging waterfalls, boiling volcanic pools, spewing 30-foot geysers, into an earthquake, avalanche and flash flood, and right through a sun-bleached dinosaur skeleton.

Fortunately for those who'd rather thrill to Big Thunder from afar, there are wonderful vantage points while sailing the Rivers of America.

Guests cruise aboard authentic reproductions of vessels that once navigated America's inland waterways. Among them are the "Mike Fink Keelboats" and two Mississippi sternwheelers of Mark Twain's era.

The lush green island rising from the Rivers of America has been claimed by Tom Sawyer for all those who dream of adventures like exploring Injun Joe's Cave or the Magnetic Mystery Mines. Guests may also visit Harper's Mill, romp across a floating barrel bridge, or fight off river pirates from inside Ft. Sam Clemens.

Accessible only by log rafts, "Tom Sawyer Island" is a particular favorite among younger guests. Elsewhere in the Magic Kingdom there are streets and sidewalks underfoot, but on the island, only grassy-edged footpaths crisscross the wilderness.

Frontier adventures abound on "Tom Sawyer Island." Rising from the untamed wilderness, Ft. Sam Clemens (below) is an outpost of civilization and well-protected haven for weary travelers.

Guests who are game for old-fashioned fun can enjoy a wild and woolly free-for-all at the "Country Bear Jamboree." In this country-western celebration, the Five Bear Rugs and Sun Bonnets, accompanied by Gomer on piano, play and sing at center stage. The velvet-draped sideboxes showcase thousands of pounds of animated "bear-itones," including Henry, the master of ceremonies, "Liver Lips" McGrowl, Terrence and Big Al.

Disney Imagineers "coach" Henry for his role as master of ceremonies in "Country Bear Jamboree," helping him to refine his dialogue and movements with Audio-Animatronics equipment. Of Henry's performance, LOOK magazine said, "His song about Davy Crockett, who 'killed him a b'ar when he was only three,' is a computerized masterpiece." Henry's fellow performers include Gomer (middle right), Zeke (right) and Trixie (far right).

Back on the mainland stands Grizzly Hall, a pine-walled Northwoods theater that is home for the "Country Bear Jamboree." In this country-western show, pioneer history takes a turn to hilarity when a bunch of foot-stompin' back-woods bruins present their "unbearably" funny repertoire of music, comedy and corn.

Among the most popular attractions in the Magic Kingdom, Country Bear Jamboree is a complete theatrical production, relying on precise timing of humorous patter and songs. And most of all, it relies on the ability of Disney Imagineers to create incredibly life-like personalities for an *Audio-Animatronics* cast that includes 17 full-sized bears, a raccoon, and the talkative hunting-trophy heads of a buffalo, stag and moose.

From nearly 60 years of experience with animated motion pictures, Disney artists have learned that a character has more believability if its gestures and expressions are understated, rather than exaggerated. For example, an animated character expresses surprise more effectively by simply raising an eyebrow, rather than throwing up its hands.

As a result, audiences at Country Bear Jamboree find themselves responding to the bears as if they were human performers. Guests sing along, applaud punchlines—and even shout for encores.

Go east from Grizzly Hall and you'll arrive at a bit of St. Louis from the 1840s. For westward-bound pioneers, this Missouri town marked the end of the civilized East and the jumping-off point for the Wild Frontier. The Diamond Horseshoe Saloon is designed after the velvet-draped dancehalls of the day, and captures the flavor of that bustling crossroads.

Here, on the border between Frontierland and Liberty Square, eastern worldliness meets western earthiness in the rollicking "Diamond Horseshoe Revue." This live stage show features "citified" can-can dancers, a rowdy frontier comic, a pistol-packing chanteuse and a dashing soldier of fortune.

Beyond the Diamond Horseshoe Saloon, the "Spirit of St. Louis" becomes the "Spirit of '76" in Liberty Square.

(Left and below) Big Al and Swingin' Teddi Barra are two of the most popular stars in "Country Bear Jamboree."

The "Diamond Horseshoe Revue" girls kick up their heels to the rousing beat of Offenbach's "Can-Can."

Liberty Square

Step onto Liberty Square and you'll walk back across the pages of American history to the Eve of Independence—1776. Here, life in the Thirteen Colonies and the Spirit of '76 have been reborn.

The blend of colonial architecture in Liberty Square includes the Dutch New Amsterdam designs of New York. The Georgian style of Williamsburg, Virginia, appears across a cobblestone street. Facing the waterfront, the buildings assume a New England character. And as one looks back toward Frontierland, there are rougher-hewn replicas of structures from the Northwest Territory.

To sample colonial hospitality, guests may visit the Liberty Tree Tavern or Columbia Harbour House. For a taste of patriotic spirit, there is a great "publick" meeting hall, echoing the colonists' challenge to "tyrannie."

Rising proudly from the village greene is the mighty Liberty Oak Tree, strung with 13 victory lanterns representing the colonies. Bordering the bustling village square are shops recalling the business life of the times, from the Silversmith to Mlle. Lafayette's Parfumerie.

(Left) Roy O. Disney chats with the "residents" of Liberty Square before Opening Day. (Below) One-of-a-kind treasures abound in the Olde World Antiques shop.

The Liberty Tree Tavern captures the warmth and hospitality of a colonial inn from the 18th century. Its windows are fashioned from handmade "seed glass," and each of its six dining areas features a unique fireplace.

(Far left) At Mlle. Lafayette's Parfumerie, guests may have individualized fragrances blended for them. Each personal scent is assigned an identification number so that it may be re-ordered by mail. The Silversmith shop offers authentic reproductions of sterling and pewter gifts in vogue during the 1700s.

The original Liberty Tree was christened in Boston in 1765, when patriots calling themselves "Sons of Liberty" gathered beneath its boughs to protest imposition of the Stamp Act. It became a living symbol of the American freedoms of speech and assembly. The Liberty Oak Tree in the Magic Kingdom is a 100-year-old southern Live Oak, quercus virginiana. Found six miles from its present home in Liberty Square, it is approximately 40 feet tall, 60 feet wide, and weighs more than 38 tons.

The tree is by far the largest living specimen in the Magic Kingdom, and probably one of the largest ever transplanted. At 38 tons,

the oak couldn't be lifted by simply wrapping a cable around it, because vital bark and cambium layers would have been damaged under so much weight. Instead, holes were drilled through the hardwood center of the trunk and steel rods inserted. The rods became grips for lifting the tree with a 100-ton crane.

The transplant not only required a good deal of skill and patience, but a heavy dose of "knock-on-wood" luck. Today, the Liberty Oak Tree looks as though it had been growing happily in Liberty Square since the American Revolution.

The "Hall of Presidents," whose steeple dominates the Liberty Square skyline, is reminiscent of the famous assembly houses found in several eastern capitals. The stately building also showcases one of the most exciting applications of the *Audio-Animatronics* system.

This Disney-engineered system of three-dimensional animation brings Magic Kingdom performers to life electronically with precisely synchronized sounds and movements. Walt Disney said the *Audio-Animatronics* system offers "the three-dimensional realism of fine sculpture, the vitality of a great painting, the drama and personal rapport of the theatre and the artistic versatility and consistency of the motion picture."

In the Hall of Presidents, the *Audio-Animatronics* system has been employed to portray the importance of the American heritage and vitality of the U.S. Constitution. The production, entitled *One Nation Under God*, leaves no guest unmoved.

A highlight of the presentation is seeing all 39 Presidents of the United States together on one enormous stage—in life-size and life-like *Audio-Animatronics* form. "From these men," we are told, "the free world may take new inspiration and hope, and new wisdom from old words of prophecy."

As a roll call begins, each Chief Executive—from George Washington to Ronald Reagan—acknowledges the announcement of his name with a modest nod or gesture, in solemn attempts not to interfere with the roll of honor.

Abraham Lincoln rises to speak for all the presidents. The words of his powerful oratory, assembled from six of his speeches, prove as prophetic today as they were when spoken more than a century ago.

While Lincoln speaks, his voice, facial expressions and body movements are kept precisely "on cue" by the *Audio-Animatronics* system. The other presidents quietly turn to each other, nod in reverence and seem to study the impact of their colleague's message upon the audience.

The overall effect is entrancing. As one guest said, "I know they can't possibly be alive, but that fact certainly does escape me now and then."

More than 15 years of work went into the "Hall of Presidents" before its debut. Sculptors alone spent two years creating life-size Audio-Animatronics figures of Presidents Washington through Nixon for Opening Day in 1971. Subsequent "inaugurations" added Presidents Ford, Carter and Reagan. (Opposite page) Authenticity was the watchword in the attraction's creation, from onstage furniture to wigs, jewelry and apparel. George Washington sits in an exact replica of his chair from the 1787 Constitutional Convention. (At left) Abraham Lincoln delivers a stirring patriotic address, created from six of his actual speeches. "All of the armies of Europe, Asia and Africa combined," he says, "could not by force take a drink from the Ohio, or make a track on the Blue Ridge."

To create realistic figures of the presidents, hundreds of paintings, photographs, films and books are studied, detailing their personalities, mannerisms and physical characteristics. (Below) Before full-size busts are sculpted, scale-size maquettes are fashioned. (Right) Painstaking attention to detail is woven into the presidential wardrobe. Veteran designers hand-tailor suits, reproducing not only the style of clothing worn by each president, but also cutting and stitching methods in fashion during each historical period.

(Left) Taking a break from the 1972 campaign trail, vice-presidential candidate Edmund Muskie stops by the "Hall of Presidents" to size up available stage space. (Below) Tip O'Neill, the venerable Congressman from Massachusetts and Speaker of the House, pauses in his 1974 visit to the Magic Kingdom to pay his respects to the"Ancients" of Liberty Square. The Ancients, a fife and drum corps, made their farewell appearance in 1980 and marched into Magic Kingdom history.

(Left) Walt Disney World pays tribute to Canada after Canadians spirit six American hostages out of Iran following the 1979 take-over of the U.S. Embassy. A special proclamation is presented to Kenneth Taylor, Canada's Ambassador to the United States, in front of the Liberty Oak Tree.

Not far from the Hall of Presidents is a residence designed to scare up some early American fantasy and folklore. High on a bluff overlooking the Rivers of America, the stone-faced "Haunted Mansion" presents the ominous spectre of a Dutch manor house from the Hudson River Valley. It's an architectural style perhaps best described as early Edgar Allan Poe.

On nights when the moon is a ghostly galleon and the sky is a cloudy sea, one might well imagine Ichabod Crane riding this way on his fateful journey through Sleepy Hollow.

A giant bat hovers above the dagger-shaped belfry. Inside the Haunted Mansion, an unbroken chain of "doom buggies" carries guests through chambers and halls equipped with wall-to-wall screams and cold-running chills.

The mansion offers a happy haunting ground and *very* active retirement for 999 ghosts, ghouls and goblins, who are just dying to take you on a frightfully funny adventure.

Eerie apparitions invade endless hallways. There's an incessant rapping on a door, but no one is there. A piano is played by unseen hands,

while the pianist's shadow bleeds across the floor.

The chanting head of a spirit medium appears within a crystal ball as spirits rise at a seance. Transparent ghosts, their feet gliding above the carpet, waltz to the strains of a spirit-possessed pipe organ in a cob-webby Grand Ballroom. Marble busts sing in the world's wildest grave-yard. And the echoes of voices are lost in the rush of a midnight wind.

Spectrally speaking, the Haunted Mansion may be a poltergeist's paradise, but for Disney maintenance crews, it's a veritable nightmare. To keep the place nice and dirty, hundreds of furnishings must constantly be covered with coats of dust, and every dark corner laced with cobwebs.

"Dust" is purchased by the pound and dis-tributed like grass seed from hand spreaders. Yet it seems to evaporate into thin air. Legend has it that since the Magic Kingdom opened in 1971, maintenance personnel have spread enough dust to *bury* the Haunted Mansion.

No one knows what strange force is behind the disappearance. The air-conditioning sys-tem, perhaps, is responsible for some of it. But as one bemused duster tells it, "There must be a witch with a broom at work in here too!"

Bidding adieu to our "ghost hosts" at the Haunted Mansion, we prepare to enter another themed land—traveling from the spirit world to the world of the future—in Tomorrowland.

Tomorrowland

Adventures on the move...around the globe and out among the stars...that's Tomorrowland. Among the experiences guests can enjoy are previewing a transportation alternative aboard the "*WEDway* PeopleMover," visiting a "Home of Future Living," racing through the cosmos in "Space Mountain," or blasting off on a "Mission to Mars."

Simply by definition, Tomorrowland poses one of the Magic Kingdom's greatest challenges for Disney designers.

In creating a Main Street, U.S.A., Adventureland, Frontierland, Liberty Square—or even the timeless world of Fantasyland—the approach is more easily defined. Design interpretations may vary, but history does not. However, Disney Imagineers recognize that because the future is a moving target, Tomorrowland must undergo continual updating.

For example, Mission to Mars was originally a "Flight to the Moon." When space exploration rocketed into new frontiers, the lunar excursion was replaced with a flight to our more distant celestial neighbor—the mysterious Red Planet.

Drawing heavily on scientific data from NASA, and on their own skills in motion-picture special effects, the Disney team took giant steps to ensure authenticity.

Along with being astronomically enlightening, the attraction is rich in light-hearted embellishments. Among them is a cosmic phenomenon that hurls passengers into a "hyper-space warp" and through an "anti-universe" mirroring their own.

Nevertheless, there can be no doubt that Tomorrowland's most stimulating sensations of space flight are inside Space Mountain.

Unveiled in 1975 after ten years in development, the gleaming white cone-shaped mountain is an engineering marvel of pre-stressed concrete and steel. It's big enough to cover a football field, and its intricate track system was designed with the aid of computers.

Towering nearly 175 feet above the ground (and descending some 15 feet below it), Space Mountain dominates the Tomorrowland skyline, housing an adventure as different from roller-coaster rides as the Magic Kingdom is from the traditional amusement park.

(Top) Disney Imagineers strove to make "Mission to Mars" as authentic as possible. In the Mission Control Center, historic NASA footage of astronauts working aboard Skylab is included in the "pre-flight preparation" show. (Above) In the main cabin of the Mission Spacecraft, passengers watch Earth fall rapidly away, as seat vibrations and subaudible waves simulate the spine-tingling sensations of lift-off. Seldom-seen close-ups reveal the surface of Mars, including photos taken by U.S. Mariner 9.

Because the rocket guideways in Space Mountain are virtually invisible during the race through space, passengers experience a sort of unanchored acceleration that seems to lift them beyond the pull of gravity. Zooming around horizontal curves and over soaring arcs, those brave enough to keep their eyes open encounter spiraling galaxies, shooting stars, meteor showers and other stellar phenomena via an ingenious process of "illusioneering." After minutes that to some space explorers seem like an eternity, rockets reenter the atmosphere and land with an other-worldly whoosh and blaze of flaming red.

Of course, one person's thrills are another's chills. And even though safety is assured at every twist, turn, dip and swerve in Space Mountain, rocketing around the universe is not for everyone.

Happily, there's another fascinating side to Space Mountain, one that the astronautically shy may explore at a more pedestrian pace. By simply sidestepping outer space, guests may explore inner space in the Home of Future Living. Here, wall-sized television screens and electronic baby-sitters are a part of everyday life.

Along with flights into outer space, Tomorrowland offers many other unique excursions, with modes of travel that are often as interesting as the destinations themselves.

Admittedly, a revolving stage might not be all that unusual. But aboard the "Carousel of Progress," the stage stays put and the audience moves. Guests revolve from the 1890s into today while experiencing a lively *Audio-Animatronics* review of electricity's growing role in the American home. Now that's progress!

In the *Circle-Vision 360* Theater, the motion picture "Magic Carpet 'Round the World" literally surrounds guests with the sights and sounds of a global tour. A Disney innovation, the motion picture is projected on a 360-degree screen.

Guests can also travel from the Magic Kingdom to other vacation ports-of-call around the world through the magic of "If You Had Wings." This ride-through adventure blends film, music, three-dimensional sets and speed-effects as in no other attraction.

Along with "Space Mountain," the "Carousel of Progress" (middle) opened at Walt Disney World in 1975. This scene depicts home electrification in the 1920s. For "Magic Carpet 'Round the World" (above), more than 37 hours of film were edited into a 21-minute journey through 20 countries. The 12-channel stereo soundtrack features a 24-voice chorus and a 56-piece orchestra, supplemented with unique folk instruments.

Scale-size race cars "compete" along the winding roadways of the "Grand Prix Raceway." Drivers of all ages are dispatched by pit attendants into four lanes of racing action, patterned after typical Grand Prix courses.

Guests pilot their "StarJets" 80 feet above
the ground, whirling around a tower styled after
a Saturn Five launch vehicle.

The inaugural run of the "WEDway PeopleMover" occurred in 1976. Unique among "people movers," the WEDway operates by a process known as linear induction. Electricity flowing through field coils embedded in the WEDway track attracts steel platens on the bases of passenger vehicles, pulling them forward. When a vehicle has passed over a given magnetized motor, the electricity in that motor switches off. The vehicle continues on, to be magnetically pulled along by other motors as it progresses down the track.

When they board the Disney-engineered *WEDway* PeopleMover, guests embark on a mile-long tour of Tomorrowland.

A state-of-the-art system, the all electric, driverless *WEDway* transports passengers along an elevated track. This not only affords excellent views, but saves the land from being carved into a roadbed. The system also spares the air from added pollution, because it relies on externally supplied electrical energy. Except for the sliding doors and wheels, *WEDway* vehicles have no moving parts. And with few parts to wear out, there are virtually no maintenance costs.

Other "people movers" are common sights in airports and shopping centers. But the *WEDway* system is unique in that the drive power is in the track, not in the vehicles. Disney Imagineers simply took an old idea, the linear-induction motor, and gave it a new application—moving people.

A more recent generation of the *WEDway* made its inaugural run at the Houston (Texas) Intercontinental Airport during 1981, the first public use of the system outside a Disney "entertainment world." It also received a commendation for design achievement from the National Endowment for the Arts and U.S. Department of Transportation.

The *WEDway* PeopleMover is just one of many forward-thinking ideas that have become real not only in Tomorrowland, but throughout Walt Disney World. Most of these technological innovations are never seen by guests. They help behind the scenes to ensure the smooth operation and high level of quality that people expect of the Disney Theme Show. Yet in many respects, what goes on behind the scenes (and in some cases, beneath the scenes) is every bit as fascinating as the Magic Kingdom's onstage experiences.

The prototype systems serving Walt Disney World, as well as its progressive building programs, demonstration projects, and high environmental standards governing development, have made the Vacation Kingdom far more than an entertainment mecca. In keeping with Walt Disney's original dream, these systems, programs, projects and standards have made the Vacation Kingdom a valuable laboratory where creative experiments in urban design can be achieved. In that sense, the real Tomorrowland is all around you.

A Walt Disney World Mark IV Monorail train glides past Space Mountain. The Monorail is one of several leading-edge transportation systems showcased in the Vacation Kingdom.

77

"City planners all over the world have for decades dreamed of urban basements like the one at Walt Disney World."

—Peter Blake, architectural editor
New York *magazine*

"Beneath the Scenes"

Conduits run along ceilings and walls in the utility corridors ("utilidors") beneath the Magic Kingdom, carrying power lines, compressed air, telephone cables, water, trash and air conditioning. When a "lifeline" needs repair, a non-polluting electric vehicle rushes workers to the trouble spot. Such accessibility is unknown in many cities, where streets must often be torn up when trouble occurs.

Many guests who stroll through the Magic Kingdom will never know that there is another world hidden just a few feet below their footsteps. For city planners and engineers, however, activities going on *beneath* the scenes are almost as spectacular as those above ground.

Excavated from the landfill foundation of the Magic Kingdom, the lower level encompasses nine acres, and is unified by more than a mile of criss-crossing "utilidors" (utility corridors). A city beneath a city, this urban infrastructure houses vital operations that keep the community above ground running smoothly.

Like the backstage area of a huge theatrical production, the lower level is a bustling place.

As many as 8,000 "stage hands" are at work there on any given day, helping to bring the Disney Theme Show to life.

The utilidors are lined with tailoring shops, make-up and dressing rooms, barbershops, employee break areas, recording and design studios, and decorating and maintenance facilities. There's also a photography lab, film studio and cafeteria.

The largest active wardrobe department in the world is housed there too. Boasting more than two million items of apparel and accessories, it features nearly 500 original costume designs for the Vacation Kingdom's 12,000 Cast members.

The costumers also provide more than 1,000 unique garments donned by the Magic Kingdom's *Audio-Animatronics* performers. The wardrobe operation is so extensive and complex (all apparel used is cleaned daily), that Walt Disney World has become a testing ground for many new fabrics introduced by American textile companies.

Perhaps the most far-sighted feature of the lower level is its advanced computer center. Aided by closed-circuit television and other communications devices, computers keep tabs on countless services across the 43-square-mile Vacation Kingdom.

Beneath the Magic Kingdom, Cast members apply makeup, change costumes, record soundtracks and perform a myriad of other backstage activities.

The Digital Animation Control System (DACS) ensures that each of the Magic Kingdom's hundreds of *Audio-Animatronics* characters will be "on cue" during their performances by orchestrating more than 72,000 individual functions every second.

During theatrical productions like Country Bear Jamboree, DACS not only gives voices and gestures to the stars, it also opens theater doors, elevates lifts on the stage, operates the lights and draws the curtains.

(Top) The main Digital Animation Control System computer room is a central maintenance dispatch center. For example, if a projector lamp burns out in the "Hall of Presidents," monitoring systems discreetly alert maintenance personnel, so that the problem can be corrected without interrupting the show. (Above) The DACS audio room houses one-inch-tape machines that each play a continuous loop of up to 14 soundtracks. The four machines in the foreground are interlocked to keep all the music synchronous for "It's A Small World."

Other DACS systems work around the clock to check environmental quality, minimize energy consumption, make hotel reservations, chill refrigerators, maintain security, provide transportation, detect smoke, or simply play music in the resort-hotel lobbies.

Malfunctioning equipment is automatically shut down, and maintenance personnel can often be warned before a breakdown occurs.

Through the utilidors, maintenance and other service personnel conduct their activities with efficiency and ease. Service vehicles never park next to Magic Kingdom shops or restaurants when unloading food or merchandise. Deliveries are made from below ground, leaving the streets above clear for pedestrians, and the peace and dreamlike quality of the Park undisturbed.

Costumed Cast members always make their onstage entrances in their appropriate themed areas. Magic Kingdom guests will never see a Tomorrowland space explorer rushing down turn-of-the-century Main Street, U.S.A., to reach his "home land."

The Magic Kingdom is ever changing, and easy access to utilities through the lower level also facilitates the introduction of new attractions and ideas—more ways to improve the overall show and guest experience.

As discussed earlier in this book, Walt Disney envisioned that his Florida project would become a showcase for the world, a "Community of Ideas" highlighting innovations from the creative centers of free enterprise, government and education.

Among city planners and engineers, one of the most popular innovations in the lower level is the Swedish-developed AVAC (Automated Vacuum Assisted Collection) trash disposal system. It is the first installation of its kind in the United States and the largest in the world.

No air-polluting garbage truck will ever hamper traffic above or below the Magic Kingdom. A network of pneumatic tubes simply whisks refuse away like magic. The trash arrives at a processing station where it is compacted and transported to a landfill site. Up to 65 tons of refuse can be handled per day.

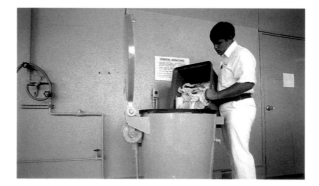

There are more than a dozen deposit stations for waste paper in the Automated Vacuum Assisted Collection (AVAC) system. Refuse is pneumatically transported to a central compactor, which automatically signals the main computer room when it's full.

The *New York Times Magazine* said—"While one could justifiably call such a system [AVAC] merely a 'pipe dream' for New York, it is, like the service tunnels, a practical possibility for new areas not yet built up."

Many more innovative technologies are being demonstrated above ground in the backstage areas of Walt Disney World.

Construction began in 1981 on a solid-waste energy conversion facility. It will feature the first commercial use of the slagging pyrolysis process. A variety of materials—including non-biodegradable ones such as rubber and plastic—will be converted into combustible gas. Heat from the non-polluting, burning gas will in turn go to boilers, helping to meet the Vacation Kingdom's hot water demands.

Natural gas has been generating a portion of Walt Disney World's electricity since 1971, by powering two jet-aircraft turbines. This Central Energy Plant was also one of the first in the United States to house boilers and absorption chillers that utilize exhaust heat. Air conditioning, hot water and heating for the Magic Kingdom and resort-hotels are by-products of the electricity production.

While the Florida sun expends much of its energy tanning sunbathers and ripening oranges, at Walt Disney World it also provides hot and chilled water, heating and air conditioning for a 70,000-cubic-foot office building.

The prototype structure has 16 solar collectors that capture the sun's rays and form the roof—an innovative, money-saving design. The building was one of 30 awarded a grant from the Energy Research and Development Agency (now the Department of Energy) for the experimental installation of solar-power systems. Reedy Creek Utilities Company, a Walt Disney Productions subsidiary, occupies the structure.

(Top left) The distribution of all utilities in the Vacation Kingdom is orchestrated at the Central Energy Plant. (Top right) Four cooling towers identify the "chiller building," where air conditioning is produced. To the left, glistening in the Florida sun, is the solar roof of the Reedy Creek Utilities Company. (Middle) Walt Disney World's solar-power project is among the most successful in a federally-sponsored demonstration program. This is one of 16 solar collectors, made up of a reflection surface and absorber. (Above) Water flowing through color-coded pipes is heated by the sun via the solar collectors. Some water also passes through absorption chillers, which remove heat for air conditioning offices in the building. The resultant hot and chilled water can be stored in tanks for three or more sunless days.

Channels of water hyacinths at Walt Disney World can remove 90 percent of the suspended particles from waste-water effluent. Hyacinths are regularly harvested and converted into soil enrichment for a nursery (shown at bottom). Effluent from a waste-water treatment plant is also sent to a percolation pond, into a wetlands-overland flow system, or to a holding pond for spray irrigation of the Tree Farm (middle right).

Waste-water treatment is effectively managed by several advanced methods at Walt Disney World.

Even after cycling through the Waste Water Treatment Plant on the Vacation Kingdom property, water still contains nutrients that would promote the growth of algae and weeds if it were returned directly to the water table. For this reason, part of the effluent is sprayed over a 145-acre Tree Farm.

The natural growth processes of the trees remove the excess nutrients from the waste water before returning it to the water table in a recycled condition. This "living filter farm" also has the spin-off benefit of accelerating crop maturation.

In a similar manner, the natural filtering properties of water hyacinths are being tested in a cooperative project with the U.S. government. These fast-growing aquatic plants not only cleanse water, but can be converted into soil-enriching mulch or methane gas, which can in turn be used to power generators.

In 1981, Walt Disney World was selected from among 200 projects to receive the Urban Land Institute Award for Excellence. This annual award "recognizes innovative land developments which embody superior design, relevance to contemporary issues and needs, and resourceful utilization of land while improving the quality of the living environment."

Environmentalists have also hailed the Disney organization for its efforts in the Vacation Kingdom. The Company has received environmental honors from the State of Florida, The American Tree Farm System, the National Society of Professional Engineers, and many other prestigious institutions.

82

The Vacation Kingdom can also "Touch '1' for First" in telephone communications. The world's first completely electronic phone company, Vista United Telecommunications (a Disney partnership), manages Walt Disney World's 12,500 phones. A computer-controlled switching system places more than two million long-distance and international calls every year, faster than and without the aid of an overseas operator.

With a history of many installation and service firsts, such as 100 percent single-party service and total touch-tone dialing, Vista United was also the first phone system to feature completely buried cable.

The phone company scored again in 1978 with the first commercial and most extensive installation of fiber-optics cable in the United States.

A laser beam sends more than 600 calls simultaneously over the fiber-optics line, which is five miles long, composed of hair-like strands of glass, and also able to transmit video. Sound quality is improved with fiber optics, and there is no interference from lightning or Florida's high water table.

The cable is one inch in diameter and has the calling capacity of a ten-inch copper carrier. Fiber-optics lines are also considerably less expensive to ship and install than conventional copper cables.

The *New York Times Magazine* called Walt Disney World "perhaps the most important city planning laboratory in the United States." Its innovative programs demonstrate that orderly urbanization *can* occur without depleting the environment.

Of course, the most enjoyable innovations for guests are still the boundless entertainment and recreational opportunities offered *onstage* in the Vacation Kingdom.

From Magic Kingdom to Vacation Kingdom

"There's enough land here to hold all the ideas and plans we can possibly imagine."

—Walt Disney

While hosting a TV news special about the opening of Walt Disney World, commentator David Brinkley said—

"It is the most imaginative and effective piece of urban planning in America. And that is totally aside from the 'Mickey Mouse' amusement park area itself. It is outside the Park, on Disney's own land, which is about twice the size of Manhattan. On this they have built roads, transportation systems, lakes, golf courses, campgrounds, riding stables, stores, hotels and so on. And they all fit together in a setting of land, air and water better than any other urban environment in America.

"We all remember seeing, years ago, those slick futuristic drawings saying what the future of the American city was going to be. Gleaming buildings, fast monorails, people in one place, cars in another. Well, this *is* the future, and none of it has happened. Nobody has done it but Disney."

As Brinkley reported, another wealth of Disney adventures awaits guests in the exciting locales surrounding the Magic Kingdom. This *Vacation Kingdom* is an entertainment world—a complete vacation resort. Its collection of unique themed environments brings to life a number of leisure-time dreams—whether it be a wish to step into the future, a yearning for the exotic South Seas, or a desire to rough it in the Great Outdoors.

Contemporary Resort Hotel

Praised for its imaginative design and dramatic use of space, the Contemporary Resort Hotel was described by the *New York Times* as "the best single building through which to observe the blending of technological innovation and far-out fantasy that is uniquely Disney."

Rising 14 stories above the shore of Bay Lake, the hotel was deliberately positioned as an architecturally compatible backdrop for Tomorrowland. This extends the theming of the Magic Kingdom beyond its borders into the resort area, with views of the Contemporary from inside the Park found almost exclusively in Tomorrowland.

Enclosed within the hotel's imposing steel and concrete A-frame is an enormous open area called the Grand Canyon Concourse. It soars nine stories and stretches one and a half times the length of a football field, with rows of guest rooms opening into it on both sides.

Sleek, silent monorail trains continually arrive and depart in this unique "lobby," transporting guests to and from the Magic Kingdom and other resort destinations.

Beneath the monorail station is a small community of shops and restaurants, set in a shimmering decor inspired by scenes of the Grand Canyon.

Colossal ceramic murals, towering like canyon walls above the concourse, are dominant design elements. Pieced together like giant jigsaw puzzles, the 54-ton murals rise 90 feet from floor to ceiling.

From design to installation as an encasement for the hotel's elevator core, the six massive panels took a year and a half to complete. They feature more than 18,000 hand-painted glazed tiles, shipped across the country from Disney's imagineering headquarters in California.

Among the performers featured at the "Top of the World" in the Contemporary Resort Hotel during the Vacation Kingdom's first decade are singers Carol Lawrence and Jack Jones, and comedienne Phyllis Diller.

The Contemporary also houses a beauty shop and health spa, and complete facilities for conventions, exhibits, meetings and banquets.

The largest convention in the Vacation Kingdom's first decade was the 26th Congress of the International Chamber of Commerce in October 1978. It was the first time the congress met outside a host nation's capital, with more than 3,000 delegates attending from around the world.

At the "Top of the World" on the Contemporary's uppermost floor, guests enjoy elegant dining, dancing, top-name entertainment and a panoramic view of the Magic Kingdom.

Just steps away from the hotel's Bayside wings are ivory-colored beaches and silvery Bay Lake. At the marina, a flotilla of watercraft is available for guest use, and cool drinks at the Sand Bar await vacationers just in off the lake or beach. For tennis enthusiasts, there are also night-lighted courts.

Walt Disney planned for the Vacation Kingdom to be "a showcase to the world for the ingenuity and imagination of American free enterprise." Certainly, the exciting innovations he envisioned were well illustrated in the construction of the Contemporary Resort Hotel.

The more than 1,000 guest rooms are prefabricated modular units that were produced at a plant three miles from the building site. At a rate of a dozen per day, assembly crews completely outfitted the eight-and-a-half-ton steel rooms with wall coverings, carpeting, mirrors, lighting fixtures, built-in furniture and elegant bathrooms.

Each guest room was then transported to the construction site, hoisted by a giant crane, and slid into the hotel's steel and concrete frame like a drawer into a bureau. With this done,

the rooms were practically ready for the housekeeper.

Because this construction method was experimental, it did not initially reduce costs. But it did speed up construction, and produced a precision finish that had not been achieved with any other prefabrication system to date.

Modular guest rooms were also used in another Walt Disney World resort hotel. But the finished product is as different in theme from the Contemporary as Adventureland is from Tomorrowland.

Near two waterfront wings of the Contemporary Resort Hotel, vacationers are tempted with everything from tennis to sunbathing to sailing.

The Walt Disney World Mark IV Monorail System is the primary link among the Contemporary Resort Hotel, Polynesian Village Resort Hotel, Guest Parking and Magic Kingdom. The monorail trains use about one-fourth the energy of autos, and transport an average of 80 thousand passengers per day, 365 days a year.

During their first ten years of service, the fleet of ten trains traveled more than five million miles, and transported more than 250 million passengers. The trains glide atop nearly seven miles of concrete guideways encircling the Seven Seas Lagoon.

With the guideways in an elevated double-loop configuration, trains pass side by side going in opposite directions, and travel as high as 65 feet above ground. Guideways cross a channel joining Bay Lake and the Seven Seas Lagoon, then pass directly through the Grand Canyon Concourse of the Contemporary Resort Hotel at the fourth-floor level.

In 1981, the Mark IV system received a commendation from the Design for Transportation National Awards Program. The program is co-sponsored by the National Endowment for the Arts and U.S. Department of Transportation, and recognizes excellence in integrating a transportation system into its environment.

By boarding a monorail train at the Contemporary Resort Hotel, it's a quick trip to our next Vacation Kingdom destination, the Polynesian Village Resort Hotel.

Polynesian Village

A secret wish to explore the romantic South Seas comes true at the Polynesian Village Resort Hotel. Resting on the shores of the Seven Seas Lagoon, this tropical "isle" is not only an ideal backdrop for Adventureland in the Magic Kingdom, but a vacation paradise as well.

The resort offers acres of white beaches trimmed with palm trees, spacious crystalline swimming pools, and a fleet of watercraft for gliding lazily along the cool lagoon. Meandering through exotic gardens, pathways connect "longhouses" filled with more than 600 guest rooms.

The Grand Opening celebration for the Polynesian Village featured a spectacular night-time luau on the lagoon shore. More than 1,000 guests feasted royally on authentic island delicacies, while dozens of Polynesian entertainers performed the native dances of Tahiti, Hawaii, Samoa, New Zealand and Bora Bora. Now, the nightly luaus in the "Polynesian Revue" at Luau

Cove are among the resort's most popular attractions.

The Grand Opening celebration concluded with an "Electrical Water Pageant" serpentining across the lagoon. Accompanied by lively music, the pageant starred King Neptune and his court of sea serpents, spouting whales, sea lions, mermaids and other creatures of the deep.

Like the Polynesian Revue, the Electrical Water Pageant is now a nightly event, gliding majestically across the waters linking the Polynesian Village and the Contemporary Resort Hotel.

Architectural inspiration for the Great Ceremonial House, the main building of the Polynesian Village, came from the royal assembly lodges once found in Tahiti.

Within the Great Ceremonial House are elegant shops, such as the Polynesian Princess and Robinson Crusoe, Esq. There's also fine dining and South Seas entertainment in the Papeete Bay Verandah. The Polynesian Village also features the relaxed atmosphere of the Barefoot Snack Bar, Tambu Lounge, Captain Cook's Hideaway, the South Seas Room, Trader Jack's Grog Hut and the Tangaroa Terrace.

South Seas performers are featured in the nightly "Polynesian Revue" at Luau Cove in the Polynesian Village Resort Hotel. (Below) The Grand Opening celebration for the resort hotel, a luau attended by more than 1,000 guests, inaugurated the nightly Electrical Water Pageant led by King Neptune.

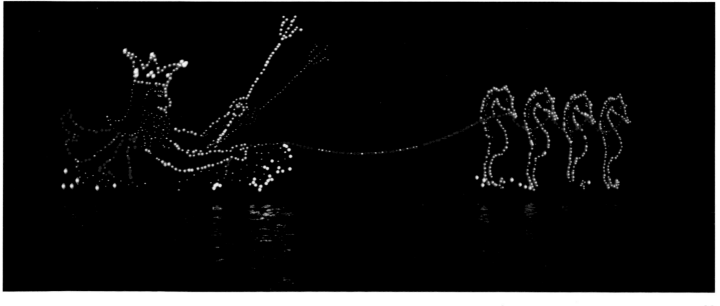

Catamarans, outrigger canoes and pedal boats are among the watercraft that sail from the Papeete Bay Marina at the Polynesian Village Resort Hotel. (Right and below) A themed swimming area at the Polynesian Village conjures up images of an enchanted island cove.

A miniature tropical rain forest flourishes within the Great Ceremonial House too. Sunlight and moonlight stream onto sprightly waterfalls, volcanic rock formations and towering coconut palms that rise to the top of a 250-square-foot atrium. This jungle features more than 75 botanic species, one of the largest indoor collections of tropic and subtropic plant life in Florida. Close to 1,500 orchids, gardenias and banana trees thrive in nearly perfect climatic conditions amongst explosions of feathery ferns.

As evidenced elsewhere in this book, Nature has always been a colorful artistic partner in rendering the Disney Theme Show. In 1955, Hollywood columnist Hedda Hopper said that to plant his "living backdrops" for Disneyland, "Walt depleted nurseries from Santa Barbara to San Diego."

In landscaping Walt Disney World, however, commercial plant suppliers were not quite so taxed. Disney horticulturalists established a 145-acre Tree Farm right on the Vacation Kingdom property.

Beginning in 1967, seeds and unrooted cuttings were brought to the farm from as far away as Australia and Africa. Young trees from

Texas, California and other states were gathered too, along with a forest-full of Florida varieties saved during site preparation and located in nearby communities.

While providing a substantial stock for Disney landscapers, the Tree Farm has also been helpful in determining what plants not ordinarily grown in central Florida could adapt to a tropical climate that sometimes experiences droughts, and is occasionally bitten by sharp frosts. This knowledge is extremely helpful in developing themed landscapes for such attractions as the Jungle Cruise in the Magic Kingdom.

As a result of their continuing research, Disney horticulturalists have succeeded in introducing many "foreign" species into the Florida plant family.

Of course, plants are only one concern of a landscape architect. Another is sculpting the soil to provide aesthetically pleasing contours. Shaping the land to create a South Seas setting for the Polynesian Village meant removing millions upon millions of cubic yards of earth. After all, what island paradise would be complete without a blue lagoon?

It was "perhaps the biggest earth-moving operation since Hoover Dam," *LOOK* magazine said, requiring nearly three years of excavation by countless workers. But as an aquatic "highway" uniting the Magic Kingdom and resort areas into a Vacation Kingdom, the Seven Seas Lagoon was well worth the effort.

As a bonus, the lagoon's creation fulfilled one of the greatest needs of the Walt Disney World construction team. It provided landfill to raise buildings above Florida's high water table. The landfill also stabilized foundations, and made possible construction of the Magic Kingdom's subterranean service facility.

In keeping with Walt Disney's directive to preserve environmental quality while building the Vacation Kingdom, nearly 1,500 trees were successfully relocated from the lagoon site to other areas of Walt Disney World.

Today the lagoon spans 185 acres, embraces three islands and reaches an average depth of ten feet. The sparkling waterway enhances the South Seas theming of the Polynesian Village Resort Hotel, offers an exciting aquatic approach to the Magic Kingdom, and is a setting for water pageants and numerous recreational activities.

Waterways of The World

(Top) The Seven Seas Lagoon during excavation, with two of its three islands visible. (Above) The Seven Seas Lagoon today. Beyond the third island, to the right of the Contemporary Resort Hotel, is the "water bridge" linking the lagoon to Bay Lake.

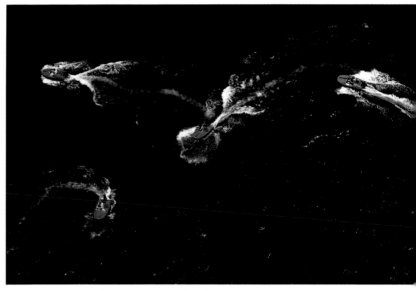

Normally a bridge is constructed to carry ground transportation over a body of water. But at Walt Disney World, a concrete "water bridge" was built *over a highway* to connect the Seven Seas Lagoon with Bay Lake, which is east of the lagoon beyond the Contemporary Resort Hotel. By crossing this unique bridge, boats have access to any number of ports, making travel around the Vacation Kingdom almost as easy by water as by land.

The Vacation Kingdom fleet features everything from 600-passenger, diesel-powered ferryboats to one-passenger, people-powered pedal boats. From the waterways of American history come two sidewheelers complete with walking-beam engines, unlike any built in the past 100 years. Walt Disney World also boasts the nation's largest fleet of pleasure craft, including sailboats and catamarans, waterskiing boats, outrigger canoes and mini-speedboats.

When Walt Disney made an aerial survey of central Florida in 1965 to find the site for his Vacation Kingdom, he flew over Bay Lake and spotted the 11-acre island near its center. Of all the locations considered, the showman said, this was the ideal spot.

(Upper left) Guests motoring on World Drive often witness an unusual scene. Boats sail over the roadway on the "water bridge" linking the Seven Seas Lagoon to Bay Lake. (Middle) Guests in mini-speedboats zip across the lake. (Above) Goofy displays his waterskiing prowess.

(Below) Discovery Island rises from the crystalline waters of Bay Lake. The white beaches at the Contemporary Resort Hotel define the lake's western shore. Just beyond the Contemporary is the Magic Kingdom, with its Main Entrance looking out onto the Seven Seas Lagoon. (Bottom) Barely off the bandstand, Guy Lombardo "takes 5" to whip around Bay Lake in a mini-speedboat during a 1977 visit.

Like the Seven Seas Lagoon, Bay Lake underwent considerable excavation before the Vacation Kingdom opened. But it wasn't to change the size or shape of the 406-acre basin. The water was simply too polluted to meet the Disney standards of "good clean fun."

Cypress swamps draining into Bay Lake for centuries had dumped vast amounts of "nutrition" for weeds and algae to feed on. Even at the surface the water was almost opaque.

To restore the lake to a pristine state meant draining three-and-a-half billion gallons of

Not all Bay Lake activities are enjoyed on the water. The shoreline offers a peaceful setting for horseback rides, and a family retreat far from the hectic pace of civilization.

water and removing an eight-foot-thick layer of muck covering the lake bottom.

But underneath all that muck was a pleasant surprise...pure white sand, which was spread along the lake shore to create beaches.

When the lake basin was refilled, it was stocked with 70,000 fingerling bass. Not only did this add fishing to the list of recreational opportunities in the Vacation Kingdom, it aided in insect control.

Today, the crystal-clear waters of Bay Lake are graced on the west by the marina and beaches of the Contemporary Resort Hotel, and on the south by another Walt Disney World resort... Fort Wilderness Campground.

Fort Wilderness Campground and River Country

The next best thing to homesteading in Frontierland is bedding down at Fort Wilderness Campground on the south shore of Bay Lake.

Ranging across nearly 650 acres, Fort Wilderness blends the rustic charm of a frontier settlement with facilities and amenities appreciated by contemporary pioneers.

Stands of ancient cypress trees bearded with Spanish moss, huge pines and white-flowering bay trees border campsites that are from 25 to 65 feet long. Each campsite integrates natural beauty with privacy in this outdoor setting.

For guests without camping gear, there are fully-equipped, air-conditioned trailers for rent in camping loops, such as Jack Rabbit Run, Terry Trail and Cinnamon Fern Way.

Fort Wilderness proved so popular after Walt Disney World's opening, the number of campsites was doubled in 1972. The following year, 300 more campsites were added, bringing the total to 825.

Campers hearing the call of the wild may join in a passel of outdoor doings. Plants and animals once seen only by Seminole Indians can be discovered along miles of winding trails on day or evening nature hikes. There are also forest pathways for jogging or bicycling.

On balmy summer nights, campers may participate in group canoe excursions featuring a marshmallow roast on shore and prime views of the Electrical Water Pageant. Power boats also set sail for romantic, moonlight cruises on Bay Lake.

Nightly campfire gatherings at Fort Wilderness offer sing-alongs with a western guitarist and screenings of Disney cartoons.

Pioneer Hall serves up the rollicking "Hoop-Dee-Doo Revue," where the antics of the Pioneer Hall Players are surpassed only by the fine home-style cookin'. There's country-fried chicken, barbequed ribs, corn on the cob, and heaps of strawberry shortcake. To wash it all down, there are bottomless pitchers of beer and sangria for mom and dad, and soft drinks for the young 'uns. Best of all, those with appetites as big as the great outdoors can have all they can eat.

Pioneer Hall, which opened in 1974, is another example of the elaborate theming at Walt Disney World. To represent a sturdy lodge of the Northwest Territory from the turn of the 19th century, Pioneer Hall was assembled with 1,283 hand-fitted logs. Florida pine trees were not tall enough, nor was their bark suitable for the two-story structure. After a six-month search, Western white pines were found in Montana and shipped by rail to Fort Wilderness. For the columns inside Pioneer Hall, 70 tons of rare ebony stone were brought in from North Carolina.

A hearty country breakfast is dished up at the Trail's End buffeteria adjoining Pioneer Hall. Campers may also pick up provisions at one of two nearby trading posts.

Themed as a lodge in the
Northwest Territory from
the turn of the 19th century,
Pioneer Hall was constructed
with 1,283 hand-fitted logs
shipped by rail from Mon-
tana. (Middle right) The
Pioneer Hall Players serve up
the wildest show of the West,
while guests enjoy hardy,
all-you-can-eat vittles during
the "Hoop-Dee-Doo Revue."

At the Settlement Trading Post, modern-day
pioneers can stock up on provisions or engage
in a leisurely game of checkers.

Trail rides in Fort Wilderness begin at the Tri-Circle-D Ranch, home for the Walt Disney World steeds. Before Opening Day, 54 saddle horses were chosen for trail rides from among more than 1,000 prospects at ranches extending from Wyoming to Oklahoma. Disney scouts spent several afternoons with each horse and its owner before final selections were made. Today, the Vacation Kingdom herd includes some of the finest trail horses in the nation.

Guests who choose not to ride can watch the meticulous daily grooming of giant Percherons, Belgians and Clydesdales after the horses return from their four-hour workdays guiding streetcars along Main Street, U.S.A.

Folks may also pay calls to the blacksmith's shop, where the vanishing arts of ironworking and horseshoeing are practiced.

Not far from the Tri-Circle-D ranch is a farm where children can pet ponies, sheep, rabbits, African pygmy goats, zebus (miniature African cattle) and other friendly critters.

(Right) Amy Carter, daughter of President Jimmy Carter, cools off at River Country on a warm August day in 1978.

And for a splashin' good time 1800s style, there is River Country. This Disney version of an old-fashioned swimmin' hole features the "Upstream Plunge," "Slippery Slide Falls," "Whoop 'N' Holler Hollow," "Raft Rider Ridge" and "White Water Rapids."

Susan Ford, President Gerald R. Ford's daughter, officially opened River Country during June 1976 by taking a slippery slide down a spiraling 260-foot water flume. Another part of the opening ceremonies had newsmen from a dozen cities adding river water from their home states to the "Ol' Swimmin' Hole."

Disney Imagineers called upon gravity to keep River Country's million gallons of water fresh in its sheltered cove.

A giant flexible tube, filled with water and monitored by a sensing device, was placed at the mouth of the Ol' Swimmin' Hole, which opens into Bay Lake. The tube expands and contracts to keep the River Country water level six inches higher than Bay Lake.

Water from the lake is pumped to the top of two giant flumes and a raft ride in River Country at the rate of 8,500 gallons per minute. Since gravity causes water to seek its own level, the River Country water spills over the top of the tube back into Bay Lake, providing needed circulation.

Such water management is an important part of Walt Disney World's operation. Indeed, water management was one of the biggest challenges in creating the Vacation Kingdom.

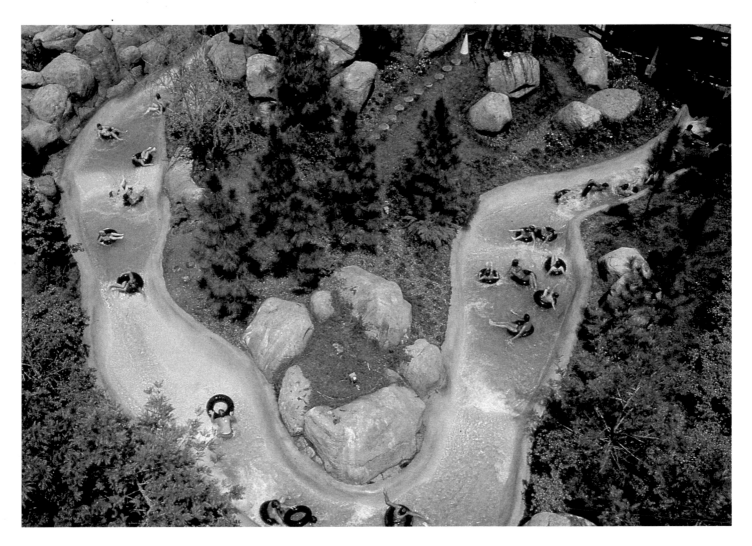

The spirit of Huck Finn is alive at River Country, where youngsters and parents together can ride the rapids, shoot down slippery slides, or simply cool off on the beach.

Environmental Planning

The many entertainment and recreation sites within Walt Disney World exist in harmony with Nature, thanks to meticulous environmental planning.

Before the Vacation Kingdom was developed, the Disney team carefully researched water-control and conservation needs. Detailed hydrological and drainage studies confirmed that before Walt Disney World could be built, major reclamation and water-control plans had to be implemented.

The Vacation Kingdom became one of the first private projects in the nation to have a sophisticated and ecologically sound plan for large-scale water control. The Reedy Creek

Improvement District, a public authority of the State of Florida, was created to undertake the program.

An initial $7.2 million effort began in 1967, and was completed in 1971. To maintain ground-water levels and keep developed areas from being inundated during rainy seasons, the water-control system uses 47 miles of canals, 22 miles of levees and 24 water-control structures.

Double-ballasted, non-powered control gates counteract Florida's typical drought-flood cycle throughout the year. They automatically float open when water reaches a peak level and automatically close when high waters subside. The natural growth of vegetation and propogation of wildlife are maintained, and life and property are protected against floods during extreme rainfalls.

Not only did efficiency and environmental impact have to be considered in creating the water-control system, but showmanship and aesthetics too. The Disney team rejected traditional straight drainage channels and insisted on natural appearing, meandering canals that accented the beauty of the land they crossed. The canals were built at considerable expense, extensively landscaped, and look and function much like natural rivers.

While the automatic gates and canals ensure that the Vacation Kingdom will never be seriously flooded, the water-control program also keeps land south of the Disney property protected.

Approximately 8,700 acres of Walt Disney World were set aside to ensure essential north-south drainage, to create a storm-water holding basin with controlled run-off, and to provide a natural conservation setting for the abundant local wildlife and vegetation.

Canal water flows to the southernmost section of the Vacation Kingdom and into the holding basin, which can handle even the most severe rainfall. Water is released slowly enough from the basin to avoid flooding outlying regions, while water levels within the conservation area are kept steady to preserve flora and fauna.

Miles of canals in Walt Disney World do more than complement natural beauty. Along with levees and other control structures, they orchestrate water levels and movement throughout the property. Aided by a holding basin, the water-management network directs drainage and protects downstream areas from floods.

(Above) Leading environmentalists from across the nation formed a Conservation Advisory Board, established in the early planning stages of Walt Disney World as part of the Disney team's environmental efforts. Board members are seen here exploring the Vacation Kingdom's 7,500 acres of conservation land. (Right) Today, the Environmental Protection Department at Walt Disney World helps shape development proposals, regularly monitors environmental quality, and manages the conservation land.

Long-range environmental planning has been paramount in all Vacation Kingdom development. Walt Disney wanted his entertainment world to demonstrate what private industry could do to preserve the ecology while building a project on land twice the size of Manhattan Island. Said one prominent conservationist, "The Disney team has followed nearly every recommendation environmentalists have made."

The original planning team for Walt Disney World included a Conservation Advisory Board comprised of leading environmentalists from across the nation. Consultation with top representatives of the World Wildlife Fund, the American Forestry Association, the Sierra Club and other organizations later led to the establishment of Walt Disney World's Environmental Protection Department. On its full-time staff are personnel trained in biology, zoology and chemistry.

The department keeps track of air and water qualities, vegetation and wildlife, and other environmental concerns. Their findings contribute greatly to the overall planning and development of Walt Disney World.

The Vacation Kingdom's construction history abounds with anecdotes about ecological preservation. For example, Disney's Environmental Protection Department discovered a grove of 125-year-old nesting trees for red-cockaded

woodpeckers on the proposed Epcot Center
site. (The birds will only nest in longleaf pines
that are at least 90 years old.) As a result, roads,
canals and other site improvements were
designed to protect and preserve the grove.

Disney environmentalists also manage the
7,500-acre conservation area. That's about
a quarter of the Vacation Kingdom property.
The land was set aside in Walt Disney World's
early planning stages as a wildlife sanctuary,
water-management area, and site for limited
ecological studies. In future years, it may
become one of the last tracts of protected wilderness in central Florida.

Insights into the lives of a remarkable assortment of flora and fauna are garnered on the
conservation land. Some trees there are several
hundred years old. The area also has a good
representation of native Florida plantlife and
several threatened and endangered animals.
More than 160 species of wild birds have been
sighted there, including the southern bald
eagle, osprey, great blue heron, sandhill crane
and swallow-tailed kite.

This protected land is a "backstage" world
that guests and even most Disney Cast members never see. But there is an "onstage"
wildlife sanctuary at Walt Disney World that
invites exploration by everyone. It's called
Discovery Island.

*The Conservation Area at Walt Disney World is so removed from
civilization, the Environmental Protection Department staff often
"listens to the silence." No din of traffic interrupts the conversing of
frogs and crickets. The area is particularly popular with such
"native central Floridians" as water birds, who live nearly as
undisturbed as their ancestors.*

DISCOVERY ISLAND

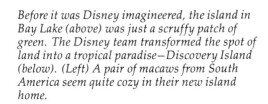

Before it was Disney imagineered, the island in Bay Lake (above) was just a scruffy patch of green. The Disney team transformed the spot of land into a tropical paradise—Discovery Island (below). (Left) A pair of macaws from South America seem quite cozy in their new island home.

A tropical haven for rare and endangered species from across the globe, Discovery Island beckons from the middle of Bay Lake. Here a rainbow of more than 500 exotic birds and unusual wild animals flourish in a verdant paradise.

Once the island was a flat, scrub-brush and vine-infested dab of sand and mud. Painstaking cultivation by Disney landscapers transformed it into an 11-acre botanical wonderland of gentle hills, misty rain forests, languid lagoons and cascading waterfalls.

The metamorphosis required 15,000 cubic yards of soil and 500,000 tons of boulders and trees. Magnolia, oak, maple, willow, cypress, and 20 varieties of palm trees formed the backdrop of greenery. To enliven the landscapers' palette, South American passion flowers and Indian orchids were imported, along with other colorful flora from South Africa, China, Japan, the Himalayas and Canary Islands.

Hundreds of brilliantly hued birds were brought in from South America, Southeast Asia, the Philippines and other faraway climes.

Pathways wind through the terrain, some carved from the soil, others fashioned out of logs connected by rope and wire-mesh bridges.

During the Vacation Kingdom's first six years, the tropical isle was called "Treasure Island," after the Walt Disney motion picture based on Robert Louis Stevenson's pirate novel. The abandoned wreck of the sailing ship *Hispaniola* still reclines on the beach today.

But as the feathered population grew and the foliage blossomed, it became clear that Treasure Island was due for a change in name and concept. The rich botanical setting had become an ideal home for rare, threatened and endangered species, and in 1978 it was renamed Discovery Island.

(Upper and lower far left) Settings from several tropic regions are recreated on Discovery Island. (Above) The wreck of the Hispaniola *reclines on the southern shore. (Left) This 300-pound beachcomber from the Pacific Ocean is one of several Galapagos tortoises, an endangered species, who reside safely on Discovery Island's Turtle Beach.*

Unlike some zoos and traditional wildlife preserves, where residents are locked up for protection, Discovery Island inhabitants are given as many opportunities as possible to roam free. The aviary netting almost seems to vanish into the foliage, and guests often don't realize that they are walking through enclosed spaces.

Among the species making their homes on Discovery Island are flocks of American flamingos and other beautiful wading birds, once nearly exterminated in their natural environments.

Colorful toucans and hornbills, whose brethren were disappearing from their jungle homes at an alarming rate, are protected on Discovery Island too. Other island beneficiaries include incubator birds, who bury clutches of eggs under piles of leaves, which they rake and attend until hatching.

Also finding sanctuary on Discovery Island are injured brown pelicans and bald eagles that cannot survive in the wild. Living alongside these creatures of the air are such earthbound animals as American alligators, giant rabbits and miniature deer. There are also flightless birds, such as ostrich-like grey rheas from South America.

While exploring Discovery Island, guests may encounter (upper right) the Patagonian cavy, a South American relative of the guinea pig; (above left) toco toucans; (above right) king vultures; (right) white crested hornbills from India; and (far right) the scarlet ibis from South America.

Wander by Bamboo Hollow and Crane's Roost and you'll come upon Avian Way. This elevated "birdwalk" winds through one of the world's largest outdoor aviaries. In its Rainbow Rookery is the most extensive colony of scarlet ibis in the United States.

These Discovery Island residents are even more brilliantly hued than their relatives in Trinidad, thanks to a special diet rich in carotenes. When perched in trees, the birds look like living Christmas ornaments.

Supplies of sticks and twigs are specially imported for the scarlet ibis from Fort Wilderness Campground, because the fussy birds won't recycle nesting materials that have been used by other fowl.

Dozens more of Nature's wonders are found around nearly every bend on Discovery Island. Among the zaniest characters are the performing cockatoos, Guinea fowl and macaws at the Coocoo Cabana. These tropical clowns are noted for personalities as colorful as their plumage. But even they can't match the grand "fowl play" perpetrated by a grey rhea named Ringo.

While sojourning at a Fort Wilderness nature preserve, Ringo swiped...and swallowed...a lady's 32-diamond antique ring.

After several traditional retrieval methods failed, Ringo went on to Tampa and into medical history when doctors performed a "ringotomy." The five-minute operation was a painless success and, after a brief recovery period, Ringo went home to Discovery Island, with his only noted side-effect being a diminished appetite for fine jewelry.

The protection and exceptionally good care of Discovery Island residents were further highlighted by the 1977 hatching of a toco toucan, the first ever bred in captivity.

Discovery Island's conservation efforts were officially recognized in 1981, when the island was made an accredited zoological park by the American Association of Zoological Parks and Aquariums.

However, for guests who are more interested in birdies than birdwatching, Walt Disney World offers a specialized resort hotel where great golf is par for the course.

GOLF RESORT HOTEL

A verdant recreational setting, the Golf Resort Hotel offers choice guest accommodations and two tree-lined 18-hole championship courses, the Magnolia (above) and the Palm (above right).

Just west of the "seaside" Polynesian Village lies the "tee-side" Golf Resort Hotel. Nestled into a quiet corner of the natural landscape, it features two 18-hole, par-72 championship courses.

Tight fairways and elevated greens, generously punctuated with water hazards and sand traps, make these courses a challenge to amateurs and pros alike.

The Golf Resort's 400 acres were carefully planned to achieve optimum golf enjoyment, ecologically-sound soil management and retention of natural beauty. The Magnolia course is lined with 1,000 magnolia trees. The Palm course is embraced by 1,000 palms in ten varieties.

Water hazards on the courses do double-duty as irrigation stores. Soil displaced from ponds and canals during construction has been used to elevate greens and tees. With some fairways raised as much as 14 feet, golfers gain unique views of entire sections of a course from its tees.

"I knew they (the courses) were going to be good," said PGA commissioner Joe Dey during Walt Disney World's opening, "but I had no idea how great until I saw them. The Magnolia is an unusually well-designed golf course."

Thanks to the luxury of space in the Vacation Kingdom, four different tees are available on all holes for flexible playing lengths. Thus golfers at varying skill levels can find sufficient challenges without frustration. Both Golf Resort courses encourage players to use nearly every club and execute almost every kind of shot.

Though shorter than the Magnolia, the Palm course is considered to be tougher. *Golf Digest* magazine placed it among "the top 100 tests of golf in America."

Yet the Magnolia course is perhaps better known. That's where the Tournament Players Association Tour (formerly the PGA Tour) plays its final round in the Walt Disney World National Team Championship Pro Am, an annual event begun in 1974. (It was a one-day Pro Am competition until 1980, when it went to a three-day Pro Am format.)

Before the team competition was established, the Walt Disney World Open was played from 1971 to 1973. Jack Nicklaus won the first of these championships with a 14-under-par 274, competing against such peers as Lee Trevino, Arnold Palmer and Billy Casper. The following year, Nicklaus recaptured his victory with a record-shattering 21-under-par 267. He scored a "triple play" with a third victory in 1973.

The challenge of championship play brings some of the most renowned competitors in professional golf to Walt Disney World, including (from top) Arnold Palmer, Jack Nicklaus and Sam Sneed. (Right) Actor Buddy Ebsen tees off in the 1977 Walt Disney World National Team Championship Pro Am. (Far right) Musical director Lawrence Welk chats with the gallery during a 1979 competition.

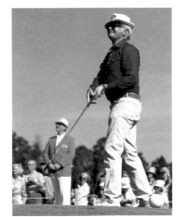

Guests wishing to strengthen their own golf games may take advantage of the Golf Resort's full-service Pro Shop. One of the services offered through the Pro Shop is the Golf Studio at the Magnolia driving range. This unique instructional program is conducted by pros for golfers of any age and at any playing level. As part of the Golf Studio experience, participants have their swings videotaped for replays and critiques in the Pro Shop.

The Palm driving range, like the one at the Magnolia, features sand traps to improve aim as well as distance. There are also two putting greens at the resort.

A special golf tournament for youth was introduced at the Golf Resort in 1977, one year after the first TPA National Junior Championship was held there. Hundreds of youths from age 6 to 17 have competed each year in the Pee Wee International Golf Tournament.

In cooperation with the TPA, Walt Disney World opened the "Wee Links" in 1980 next to the Magnolia course. For a nominal fee, a beginning golfer receives rental equipment, one lesson, and unlimited use of this unique 6-hole, 23-acre course, with holes ranging from 90 to 280 yards.

The Wee Links were designed with youngsters especially in mind, as a means of teaching golf fundamentals. It is the hope of Walt Disney World that the easy-to-build, low-maintenance course will become a model for communities wishing to establish programs for junior players.

(Top left) The Pro Shop at the Golf Resort Hotel offers a full complement of equipment and services. (Top right) Participants in the Golf Studio have their swings videotaped at the Magnolia driving range. (Middle) The video tape is replayed in the Pro Shop, where participants' techniques are analyzed and critiqued. Each Golf Studio participant receives a personal audio cassette, restating suggestions offered during the program. (Above) Developing talent from potential was a key goal in creating Walt Disney World's junior golf program. The Pro-Junior Golf Tournament, an annual event held on the "Wee Links," brings recognition to young golfers and seeks to encourage a life-long interest in the sport.

When guests take breaks from the greens at the Golf Resort Hotel, they can enjoy leisurely afternoons on their patios or balconies, invigorating sets of tennis, or cooling dips in the hotel's swimming pool.

The Golf Resort was originally planned to be a country club, where guests could play during the day, while staying overnight elsewhere in the Vacation Kingdom. However, due to the interest of golfers in having a resort world of their own, hotel accommodations were added in 1973. Today, the cozy wood and volcanic-stone clubhouse features 151 guest rooms, each with a pleasant view and enough peace and quiet to soothe even the most savage duffer.

Guests can relax on their balconies and patios, or dine in the comfortable Trophy Room. With the added offerings of swimming, tennis, and complimentary transportation around Walt Disney World, this golfer's paradise becomes a vacation delight for the whole family.

The challenge of sinking a birdie putt often brings players to yet another course in the Vacation Kingdom. This par-72 beauty is the perfect complement for a unique vacation settlement...the Walt Disney World Resort Community of Lake Buena Vista.

The Resort Community of Lake Buena Vista

The Walt Disney World resort community of Lake Buena Vista offers a healthy assortment of recreational activities, shopping and dining experiences, conference settings, guest services and lodgings.

Existing comfortably with Nature, the community was blended into a wooded 4,000-acre site in the southeastern corner of the Vacation Kingdom.

Guest accommodations were designed for those who dream of a peaceful retreat beside a lush rolling fairway or a secluded hideaway near a sun-spangled lagoon. Luxurious lodgings are found in a variety of settings at the Vacation Villas, Treehouse Villas, Club Lake Villas or Fairway Villas.

Even more spacious than the resort-hotel guest rooms, most of the Villas feature separate living rooms and kitchens. But the Villas are more than merely attractive and spacious. They are proof that beautiful and efficient housing can be harmonious with the environment.

Perched among the pines along the Lake Buena Vista Golf Course, the two-bedroom Treehouse Villas illustrate a novel way to build residences in wetlands. Resting atop ten-foot-high pedestals, the Treehouses would stand above flooding if there were sufficiently heavy rainfall, leaving the ground below clear for natural drainage. The octagonal homes also boast marvelous bird's-eye views of their natural surroundings.

(Above left) The Club Lake Villas. (Above and at left) The Treehouse Villas are nestled into secluded natural settings, with some Villas looking out onto the Lake Buena Vista Golf Course or winding canals.

(Above) The Fairway Villas are just an easy stroll away from the Lake Buena Vista Club (below), the site of tennis, golf, swimming and fine dining.

Designed to showcase energy-efficient housing ideas, the Fairway Villas benefit from thoughtful positioning and energy-conserving construction methods and materials.

Exaggerated roof overhangs and double-glazed windows reduce heat absorption through exterior walls during warm weather. Air-to-air heat pumps serve as energy-minded air conditioners. When an air conditioner is on, heat is recovered from its condenser to provide hot water.

To preserve the major portion of the surrounding acreage for parks and recreation, Disney planners clustered the Lake Buena Vista Villas around heavily wooded courtyards and cul-de-sacs. Planners avoided the "grid" system found in many neighborhoods, where residences are uniformly built on rows of small, square subdivided lots.

Most of the Villas look out onto natural surroundings, rather than onto other dwellings. Thus, clustering not only saves more space for recreation, it retains a sense of privacy while enhancing the spirit of community.

By just stepping out of a Villa door, a jogger can begin a brisk run down a tree-lined pathway, or a bicyclist may take a leisurely spin along eight miles of specially designed trails. There are also three swimming pools that offer cool respites from a summer day.

Within walking distance of the Vacation Villas is the Lake Buena Vista Club. Along with its own swimming pool and three night-lighted tennis courts, this recreation center boasts the par-72 Lake Buena Vista Golf Course, replete with a Pro Shop and locker rooms.

Designed with mid-handicap players in mind, the Lake Buena Vista course is still challenging enough to be included on the TPA Tour (Tournament Players Association, formerly the PGA). The Lake Buena Vista Club also features one of the finest gourmet restaurants in central Florida.

Not far from the Lake Buena Vista Club is the Conference Center, opened during spring 1980. This 8,000-square-foot facility was designed expressly for small to medium-sized meetings and seminars. Movable walls in the cedar-covered, chalet-style building allow the four main rooms to be configured in several ways. When the rooms are combined into one 6,500-square-foot space, more than 500 guests may be comfortably seated theater style.

The Conference Center also features advanced lighting, sound and audio-visual systems, and can handle television broadcasts, press events and multi-media shows. With the added 30,000 square feet of convention space at the Contemporary Resort Hotel, groups of nearly any size may be hosted at the Vacation Kingdom.

The exceptional guest accommodations, services and recreational opportunities at Walt Disney World prompted the readers of *Meetings and Conventions* magazine to rank the Vacation Kingdom among the nation's top meeting centers for the last three years.

The Hotel Plaza in Lake Buena Vista has four major independently owned and operated hotels, each offering its own collection of recreational activities.

Near the Hotel Plaza, at the heart of the resort community, is the treasury of charming waterfront shops, boutiques and restaurants of Walt Disney World Village.

The Empress Lilly *riverboat, with its elegant cargo of fine restaurants and lively lounges, is a gleaming centerpiece among the shops, boutiques and other restaurants of Walt Disney World Village. Beyond the Village, to the left, are the high-rise lodgings of the Hotel Plaza.*

As one would expect, nothing about the Village is ordinary. The chrome and concrete architecture typical of many shopping complexes has been forsaken here. In its place are weathered bricks, rich woods and cedar-shingles that engender a warm and intimate atmosphere.

Exhaustively landscaped and embracing the 35-acre Buena Vista Lagoon, the Village reflects the same keen sense of design continuity found throughout the Vacation Kingdom.

But while the Village is harmonious, it is hardly homogenized. Each shop is stocked with its own pleasant surprises, and every restaurant and lounge is flavored with distinctive design accents.

Included among the shops are the Great Southern Craft Company, Toys Fantastique, Country Address, Sachet In, 24K Precious Adornments, and Lillie Langtry's Old-Fashioned Photo Studio.

Among the dining facilities are the Verandah Restaurant, Cap'n Jack's Oyster Bar, Heidelberger's Deli, Lite Bite and the Village Restaurant.

Adjoining the Village Restaurant is the comfortable Village Lounge. Outfitted with cushy low sofas and club chairs, it presents the kind of jazz performers usually found only in big cities. It's a great spot for before- or after-dinner drinks.

(Middle left) Port of Entry, offering a bounty of imported gifts, is one of many distinctive shops in the Walt Disney World Village. (Above) Diners enjoy views of languid Buena Vista Lagoon from the Village Restaurant.

On any day, a host of skilled artisans is found at the Village practicing vintage trades, from cutting crystal to shaping pottery to engraving gold. But during the "Festival of the Masters," held every autumn, the Village overflows with a cornucopia of art and crafts from nationally known talents.

More than 200 artists from across the country (all winners of major shows) display paintings, photographs, sculpture and ceramics at the festival. Among the most popular events in the Vacation Kingdom, the festival debuted when the Village opened in 1975.

"The Glory and Pageantry of Christmas" is another annual Village tradition. On Christmas Eve in the year 1280, a small village in southern France honored Jesus Christ's birth with simple gifts brought to a Nativity scene in the village square. That ceremony is recreated at Walt Disney World Village.

The imagination and intense concern for guest convenience that went into planning the rest of the Vacation Kingdom is also evident in the Village.

While some guests arrive at the Village in their own vehicles, they leave them in parking areas on the perimeter and proceed on foot. Like the Magic Kingdom, the Village is a walker's paradise.

Buildings are artfully grouped in a horseshoe shape around Buena Vista Lagoon. Numerous shaded benches and outdoor cafes encourage guests to slow down, relax and enjoy the peaceful atmosphere.

(Top right) The "Festival of the Masters" at Walt Disney World Village. (Above) "The Glory and Pageantry of Christmas."

To some, the presence of an ornate 19th century Mississippi sternwheeler might at first seem unusual in an informally styled, contemporary shopping village. Yet, just as Cinderella Castle looks welcome at the end of the Victorian-styled Main Street, U.S.A. in the Magic Kingdom, the *Empress Lilly* riverboat seems to belong among the "buena vistas" of Walt Disney World Village.

Named after Walt Disney's wife Lillian, the riverboat was christened in 1977. A sparkling centerpiece for the Village, the 220-foot-long vessel has graceful lines that infuse its surroundings with the elegance of a more genteel era.

Designed by Disney Imagineers, the *Empress Lilly* is an original, combining time-tested elements of a century-old showboat and a steamboat.

Authentic features include two towering smoke stacks and "hog chains," which stretch between two slanted poles that climb from the hull to the third deck. On older, flat-bottomed vessels, these hog chains kept the middle from sagging under heavy cargo, while preventing the stern from sinking under the weight of a paddle wheel, boiler or engine.

Inside the *Empress Lilly* are flowered carpets, etched glass, tufted Victorian love seats, brass fixtures and dainty curtains. Honduras mahogany gleams throughout interior hallways and gently accents the Empress Room, one of three fine restaurants on board.

The Empress Room is appointed in Louis XV decor, creating a warm and elegant atmosphere. Some of the room's elaborate moldings are even covered in 14K gold leaf.

Next door in the Empress Lounge, the riverboat's luxurious atmosphere is heightened by the romantic strains of a harp.

Hearty steak dinners are served in the Steerman's Quarters on the main deck. The Fisherman's Deck is a seafood restaurant with curved glass windows, affording a 180-degree panoramic view of Buena Vista Lagoon.

In the lively Baton Rouge Lounge, the finest in Dixieland jazz is a regular event. And each morning, guests meet favorite Disney characters while breakfasting aboard the riverboat.

The Village Marina offers other "boating" opportunities. Little motorized "water sprites" can be rented to skim the tree-lined canals behind the Vacation Villas and the Lake Buena Vista Golf Course. Paddle boats are available for more leisurely, self-propelled journeys. A 16-foot-long canopy boat seats up to ten adults for an afternoon picnic. And those who would rather relax and let someone else do the sailing may charter boats accommodating up to 18 people.

Like the Seven Seas Lagoon, Buena Vista Lagoon was Disney engineered. Primarily excavated for water control, it is also an excellent travel lane. Guests enjoy easy access by boat to almost all developments within the Lake Buena Vista resort community.

Along with the waterway, pathways and trails for non-polluting electric carts, bicycles and pedestrians are the "main streets" of Lake Buena Vista.

Far from being a casually conceived design, this traffic pattern is central to the community's master plan. From the beginning, Disney planners sought to immunize Lake Buena Vista against the all-too-common problem of traffic congestion by developing an internal circulation system that encouraged other modes of transportation.

The placement of parking areas for guest

vehicles in peripheral locations was an important part of master planning all of Walt Disney World. When a guest arrives—whether for a day or an entire vacation—there's never a need to use personal transportation. Monorails, ferryboats, buses and trams move guests easily and conveniently throughout the Vacation Kingdom.

The Walt Disney World transportation system is perhaps not only more convenient, efficient and pollution-free than a guest's personal vehicle, it's probably a lot more fun. Colorful, comfortable and most accommodating, the Vacation Kingdom vehicles and watercraft make it easy for guests to spontaneously take off to any Walt Disney World destination almost whenever the spirit moves them.

As the Vacation Kingdom grows, so will its transportation system. The Monorail loop linking the resort hotels with the 12,000-car guest-parking area and the Magic Kingdom was designed for expansion. In the Vacation Kingdom's second decade, the Mark IV monorail trains will glide along a new seven-mile route, bringing guests to the Newest Wonder of Walt Disney World... Epcot Center.

Epcot Center

The Dream Comes True

On October 1, 1982, when Walt Disney World's year-long "Tencennial" celebration ends, the 21st century begins. On that date Epcot Center debuts, a blend of advanced technologies and showmanship as far advanced from the Magic Kingdom as Disneyland was from the old-fashioned amusement park.

Epcot Center celebrates human achievement and potential. Its foundation is Walt Disney's great dream for a community of ideas and nations. Its keystones are the master showman's boundless optimism and faith in people.

Promising ideas for enriching life will continually be previewed in the entertainment adventures of Future World, one of Epcot Center's two major areas. Included in Future World's plan are Spaceship Earth, Universe of Energy, World of Motion, Journey into Imagination, The Land, Horizons, The Living Seas, Epcot Computer Central, the Travelport and many more leading-edge attractions.

World Showcase, Epcot Center's second major area and the first exposition of its kind, brings nations together in friendship to share accomplishments and cultures. Represented on Opening Day will be Canada, China, France, Germany, Italy, Japan, Mexico and the United Kingdom. The American Adventure will be the host pavilion.

Like all of Walt Disney World, Epcot Center will always be in a state of becoming. More nations will join the World Showcase after Opening Day. And Future World will be everchanging to embrace the constant flow of innovations that follow a moving target called tomorrow.

(Above) Spaceship Earth stands at the Epcot Center entrance in Future World. The 164-foot "geosphere," the first structure of its kind, houses a ride-through experience retracing the evolution of human communications from cave drawings to satellites.
(Below) A new "Eiffel Tower" rises above boulevard shops filled with fine china, wine and perfumes at the France pavilion in the World Showcase. Whisking guests across the French countryside, an unparalleled film experience is underscored by soaring romantic music from France's great composers. And for a true "taste of France," guests may dine in a restaurant hosted by renowned French chefs.

Walt Disney once said...

"You can dream, create, design and build the most wonderful place in the world, but it requires people to make the dream a reality."

Our thanks go to the 126 million guests who helped make Walt Disney World's first decade of dreams come true...and to all those whose dreams will shape the future.